BEST PRACTICES

in Law Firm Business
Development and Marketing

BEST PRACTICES

in Law Firm Business Development and Marketing

Deborah B. Farone

Practising Law Institute • New York City • #241493

QUESTIONS ABOUT THIS BOOK?

If you have questions about billing or shipments, or would like information on our other products, please contact our **customer service department** at info@pli.edu or at (800) 260-4PLI.

For any other questions or suggestions about this book, contact PLI's **editorial department** at plipress@pli.edu.

For general information about Practising Law Institute, please visit www.pli.edu.

Legal Editor: Lori Wood

LCCN: 2018938490

ISBN: 978-1-4024-3116-6 (casebound)
ISBN: 978-1-4024-3270-5 (softbound)

For my parents Henry and Phyllis Brightman.

To my mom, for allowing me to test my wings,
even though my feet could never navigate a balance beam,
and to my dad, for exhibiting the purest form of
ethics, compassion and wonder throughout his life.

About the Author

Deborah Brightman Farone has served as chief marketing officer at two of the world's most successful law firms, Cravath, Swaine & Moore LLP and Debevoise & Plimpton LLP. At both firms, she built and led their marketing communications and business development departments. Farone has also held positions as a marketing specialist at two global advisory firms, Willis Towers Watson and Ketchum. In 2017, she launched her own consulting practice, Farone Advisors LLC, where she advises leading law and other professional service firms on business strategy and marketing. www.deborahfarone.com

Farone was nominated by her peers as the first recipient of the Legal Marketing Association's Legacy Award in recognition of her contribution to the profession. She has lectured throughout North America and in Europe and has served on the adjunct faculty of New York University. Farone and her husband live in New York. In her spare time, she can be found taking photographs throughout Manhattan.

Table of Chapters

Table of Contents

Acknowledgments

Once I committed to writing this book, I knew there was no looking back. I mapped it out as I would any other project. I broke it down into what I thought were the right steps (I was almost right), and began to set up the interviews.

My first interview was with the founder of the *American Lawyer*, Steve Brill. It was a bit intimidating, but Steve's candor and encouragement set the momentum for the more than sixty interviews that would follow. I knew this was going to be a challenge, but I had already jumped into the deep end and would have to figure my way out from there.

I realized in writing this book that there are many incredible professionals with their own unique perspectives on legal marketing. In order to provide the best view on what is happening today and to include ideas and tools with the greatest value for the future, I went to those whom I believe had great insights and stories to tell. My hope is that I could consolidate some of that thinking in one place, so that it could be helpful to lawyers managing the marketing function, marketers serving as catalysts for change, and the consultants who work within the profession.

One thing I have learned throughout this process is that we still have a lot to learn from one another. There is no way to cover everything that is impacting legal marketing, particularly in one book. I have, however, tried to cover those topics and speak with those people where I thought there was the greatest potential to provide insight and guidance.

The book would not have been possible without a lot of help, actually, a profession-full of help. I am enormously grateful to all of those chief marketing officers, law firm leaders, consultants, general counsel, and other innovators who helped me in this process. They put up with long interviews, a slew of prying questions, and in many cases, lots of back and forth. There were several others whom I had hoped to interview, particularly those who cover the profession through podcasts, blogs, and other means. Many of them are shaping the profession today. I knew that I could never tell the whole story. I leave it to others to cover the rest.

The members and leadership of the Legal Marketing Association were incredibly supportive, and I can't think of a better professional organization in which to be involved. My thanks to Liz Cerasuolo, Betsi Roach and Cynthia Voth for their information and encouragement.

I thank my husband, Dr. Egidio Farone, for making me trust my instincts and for being at my side. And a big thank you to my sister, Dr. Rebecca Brightman, for showing me how to be brave and always pointing me toward the place where I could find emergency chocolate or an extra boost of confidence.

To my family, Josh, Sam, and Bruce Altman; Raffaela DiStasio and Josephine Tarulli and their spouses and children, thank you for all of your good humor and support.

My sincere thanks go to those who provided insights through their interviews and the special "Think Pieces" I've placed at the end of most chapters. My hope is that by providing the reader the chance to hear from other voices, it would keep the book both interesting and honest. Thank you to those who allowed me to harvest written content and for all those who agreed to be interviewed: Ida Abbott, Guy Alvarez, Jeff Berardi, David Bernstein, Amanda K. Brady, Connie Brenton, Steven Brill, David Burgess, Kristin Calve, Bill Carter, Yolanda Cartusciello, Bonnie Ciaramella, Tim Corcoran, Silvia Coulter, Darryl Cross, Lara Day, Katrina Dewey, Jamie Diaferia, Susan Saltenstall Duncan, Sally Feldman, Ralph Ferrara, Dyan Finguerra-DuCharme, Jeff Franke, Heidi Gardner, Lee Garfinkle, Pierre Gentin, Rieta Ghosh, Ann Lee Gibson, Mark Greene, Carol Greenwald, Robert Gunderson, Despina Kartson, Sanjay Kamlani, Jeffrey Klein, Robert Lennon, Natalie

Loeb, Catherine Alman MacDonagh, Stefanie Marrone, Charles Martin, Catherine McGregor, Michael Mills, Steve Naifeh, Henry Nassau, Kevin O'Keefe, Allen Parker, David Perla, Aric Press, Bob Rowe, Norm Rubenstein, Jennifer Scalzi, Reena SenGupta, Stephanie Scharf, Silvia Hodges Silverstein, Tim Smith, Steven Spiess, Andrew Stamelman, Adam Stock, Daniel Troy, Alexandra Walsh, Beth Wilkinson, Barry Wolf and Mitch Zulkie.

In addition to my immediately family, I thank my other "family," those friends and colleagues who through their friendship, support, and belief made this work possible. Thank you to Sam Butler, Evan Chesler, Greg Furman, Jim Goodale, Brian Houk, Michael Mellor, Renee Miller-Mizia, Linda Orton, Terri Roth, Carolyn Sandano, Randall Smith, Robin Stamelman, Cathy Stevenson and Susan Weinberger.

And to the wonderful people at PLI who collaborated on the project, a special thanks to Anita Shapiro, Lori Wood, Ellen Siegel, and David Smith. Thank you to Melanie Stamelman, Aleah Whitten and Miriam Holzman Sharman, my swat team of grammarians.

Lastly, to all of the marketers at law firms, continue to have the strength to know that even during the toughest times, you are leading a path to the future. Believe in yourself.

"And above all, watch with glittering eyes the whole world around you because the greatest secrets are always hidden in the most unlikely places. Those who don't believe in magic will never find it."

—Roald Dahl

Chapter 1

Opening the Boxes of Best Practices

Our First Few Steps

September 28, 1989. It had been a year of change. The Berlin
wall was being dismantled, Ronald Reagan was completing his term
in the White House and the tanker Exxon Valdez spilled 11-mil-
lion gallons of crude oil in Alaska, prompting the greatest human-
caused environmental disaster of its time. And British computer
scientist Timothy Berners-Lee was creating the first web browser.

As the two of us quickly walked down the corridor, Rachel
Dressler, the firm's director of HR, was upbeat as she chatted to me
about how "unbelievably super-smart" the lawyers were with whom
I would be working. We were on the twentieth floor at 875 Third
Avenue in the center of New York City. The floor housed the busy
hub of Debevoise & Plimpton LLP's tax department and the home
of the firm's steno pool, the name given to the group of secretaries on call to help with the lawyers' overflow document processing
needs. Rachel brought me to a small windowless office that had
been taken over just a few years earlier to be used as a storage closet
for firm-related memorabilia.

The office was filled with large caramel-colored boxes, stocked with newspaper clippings, back editions of the firm's in-house newspaper *The DebeVoice*, old worn photographs and a few dated documents that appeared to detail plans for a brochure celebrating the firm's Paris office. There were the office basics: a chair, a desk, a phone, a computer, a large empty rolodex, and a typewriter. Rachel provided me with helpful information as she spoke in rapid-fire detail about the firm's policies, the lawyers' practices, and acceptable office attire. And then she offered that if I ever became busy, the steno pool might be able to assist me. But that, she reminded me, was only the case if they were not already consumed with the lawyers' work.

Alone in the office and rummaging through the boxes, I found a striking black and white glossy photograph of a lawyer whom I would later learn was Francis T.P. Plimpton, one of the firm's early name partners. In the photo, Plimpton looked as if he was perfectly posed for an ad, perhaps for one selling the services of a private bank. He was distinguished in a Christopher Plummer sort of way, with a dusting of light grey hair, properly lined crow's feet at his temples and glasses resting on his forehead, as if he was getting ready to inspect the inner workings of a watch, or a tiny insect that had fallen on top of a document. His expression in the photograph seemed to say one thing to me: *Betcha can't do this.*

I was off to the races with a career in law firm marketing.

Being the first marketer at Debevoise was an exciting and yet somewhat overwhelming task. I was twenty-six years old. My first exposure to law firm marketing came a few years earlier, when the law firm Milbank, Tweed, Hadley & McCloy LLP hired Ketchum, the PR agency where I held an entry-level job. In those days, there were only a handful of us in marketing roles around the country who knew the words "law firm" and "marketing" could coexist in the same sentence. I had moved from Ketchum to Towers Perrin (now Willis Towers Watson), and left Towers when I was recruited by Debevoise.

While my first office might not have been ideal, the partners who hired me were. That made the journey well worth it. Our presiding partner, the firm's name for its senior-most partner, and one of the three partners involved in hiring me, was an intelligent and visionary man, Bill Matteson. Bill, who had assumed the leadership role just two years before I was brought in to the firm, was considered ahead of his time. He believed that law firms needed to connect more closely with the outside world and that they should operate like businesses. Bill felt the time had come for the firm to hire some type of marketing or communications professional and assigned the task of finding the "some type" person to the sharp and irreverent media and First Amendment pro Jim Goodale. In Jim's former life, he had served as General Counsel of the *New York Times* and later as its Vice Chair. He had a great professional sense of how far he could push the envelope in terms of both the firm's culture and in terms of helping his clients. While at the *Times*, Jim had been involved in four Supreme Court cases that helped shape modern First Amendment law.

Once I was offered the job by Bill and Jim, the details involved in the position were ironed out with a third partner, Bill's soft-spoken deputy and the leader of the firm's tax practice, Phil Winterer.

Bill quickly became my mentor and a confidant whenever I faced significant issues, but I was aware that I was not the only one benefitting from his advice and his kindness. Several others within the firm, including Franci Blassberg, a first-class mergers and acquisitions partner, had also been taken under Bill's wing. Because of those relationships, Franci would make sure that I was brought into the right partner meetings and became integral in practice group discussions. That is something for which I will always be grateful.

I believe that part of Bill's passion for running the firm like a business was sparked by working with corporate clients, including Lee Iacocca, the leader of Chrysler. Bill had worked closely with Iacocca and served as the lead attorney on the company's historic rescue mission, the 1979 bailout.

Bill believed in looking to corporations for management inspiration. Like any other business, he believed that business development needed to be incorporated as a discipline, just like financial controls and leadership accountability.

Bill was also one of the best client relationship role models for which anyone could have dreamed. He was known for saying "Make your clients your friends and your friends your clients." It was a truism that many of us who worked with him believed was possible. Bill was constantly networking and socializing with people, inside and outside of the legal profession. He would extend himself to work with clients at any time of the day or night, but I quickly learned never to plan a meeting with Bill on a Monday morning. That was the golden time set aside for his weekly tennis game with his best friend, Sam. Sam, I would later learn, was Sam Butler, the leader of Cravath and someone with whom I would eventually work.

During my first years at Debevoise, I occasionally heard about other law firms in New York City that were hiring marketing people. There were just a few of us in those days; Milbank, Tweed, Hadley & McCloy LLP; Cleary Gottlieb Steen & Hamilton LLP; Simpson Thacher & Bartlett LLP; and Skadden, Arps, Slate Meagher & Flom LLP, were home to some of the first ones. Somehow, we marketers found one another and introduced ourselves. Like people stuck together in the dark, we were feeling around for a handrail. Every few months we would meet for a quick lunch. The goal of our informal network was a simple one: we wanted to be there to support one another. Whenever possible, we served as a sounding board for each other's challenges and applauded ourselves for the successes that came from being involved in winning a piece of new business, or receiving approval to hire an assistant. Even today, though there are more people involved in legal marketing, the community of law firm marketers is a close-knit one. While there are competitive topics we are unable to discuss, we try to be there for one another in whatever way possible. In those days, now more than two decades ago, we would compare notes on how to cajole other administrative staff, particularly the secretaries, legal assistants and receptionists, to help us with rudimentary work, such as getting the requisite client mailings into the mail or checking the phone numbers for a client database. We would discuss best practices in order to figure out what the local bar rules might be for handling marketing in various jurisdictions around the world. Our biggest challenge, which somewhat remains today, was how to convince lawyers who were reticent to market that it could make a difference in shaping their practice and retaining clients. Our jobs were demanding, many of the partners seemed wary, and the field of law firm marketing was new. Still, we were a resilient group and we embraced the challenging situation we faced.

In other parts of the country, particularly in Chicago and California, an industry group was sprouting. In 1985, an organizing meeting of a dozen law firm marketing people was held in San Francisco, and in 1986, the National Association of Law Firm Marketing Administrators (NALFMA), was launched. NALFMA was comprised of a small group of legal marketers venturing out into the unknown. Chapters of the national organization began to spring up across the country, and today, there are 3,900 members in twenty-five countries. The group rebranded itself in 1998 as the Legal Marketing Association (LMA).

The Rise of Legal Advertising and Legal Media

Profound developments in the legal profession in the late 1970s paved the way for the emergence of the legal marketing industry. In 1977, a U.S. Supreme Court case, *Bates v. State Bar of Arizona*, 433 U.S. 350 (1977), lifted the ban on attorney advertising. That was followed by the creative force of Steven Brill, who ushered in the new era of law firm marketing by forcing law firms to operate with greater transparency and more like public companies rather than groups of tradesmen. In 1979, Steven started the *American Lawyer* and later went on to amass a ring of ten regional legal publications.

Those years, between 1977 and 1979, changed the landscape for legal marketing, legal media, and law firm management.

"All of the firms wrote the exact same thing in their letters. While the letters were typed, each on their own different letterhead, they all said that they would offer students a unique and special experience, a unique and wonderful chance to work on unique and unusual matters."

—Steven Brill, Founder of the *American Lawyer*

Steven's inspiration for covering law firms as a business arose while he was a student at Yale Law School. At that time, law firms marketed themselves for recruiting purposes by preparing lengthy letters describing the opportunities at their firms.

"While at Yale, I was hanging around the spot where they kept the soda machines. I saw several letters posted on a bulletin board, each one from a different law firm, each one describing why students should interview there."

It was then he noticed something odd. "All of the firms wrote the exact same thing in their letters. While the letters were typed, each on their own different letterhead, they all said that they would offer students a unique and special experience, a unique and wonderful chance to work on unique and unusual matters. Basically, they were all saying the exact same thing. It's just that those words offering unique experiences were appearing on different pieces of letterhead."

Steven, who was a working journalist, writing for *New York Magazine* while attending law school, decided that he would write about the legal profession. He knew that there were aspects of the profession that made it interesting and that it was impossible that all of these firms could be exactly alike. Steven recognized that it was a profession that had not yet been covered (or uncovered) by the press.

In 1976, he wrote a watershed piece in *New York Magazine*, "Two Tough Lawyers in the Tender-Offer Game." It was one of the first significant pieces of journalism to uncover the inner workings of the corporate legal profession. The piece told the story of two young lawyers, Joe Flom of Skadden, and Marty Lipton of Wachtell, Lipton, Rosen & Katz, who were pioneers in the world of mergers and acquisitions.

As he continued to cover the legal profession, Steven's profound impact on it was at least twofold: he forced law firms to think of themselves more like corporations, pressuring them to start reporting revenue figures and develop a new metric — profit per partner; and he trained legions of reporters to ask the toughest questions of law firm partners.

There were a handful of other journalists who helped tell stories of what was taking place in the legal world. David Margolick was the legal affairs reporter for the *New York Times*, and his weekly "At the Bar" columns were widely read every Friday. Jerry Finkelstein also was well known in political and news circles and as the publisher of the *New York Law Journal*.

And Suddenly, We Multiplied

Since the early days of legal marketing and legal media, we've seen the profession explode, with the success of numerous publications covering the law, the proliferation of rankings, and the battle among firms to differentiate themselves by building better websites, creating pitch materials, and utilizing business, competitive and even artificial intelligence. Today's large law firms, particularly those that are super-regional, national or global, may have sales teams, sophisticated account-management programs, client-feedback plans, and pricing professionals who are adept at financial modeling the cost for a legal engagement. Lawyers at all-size firms have discovered the use of hiring outside coaches and the value of connecting with the outside world through social media, including blogs, LinkedIn and Twitter.

But marketing does not occur in a vacuum. Along with changes to the way firms promote themselves, there have been significant changes in the way firms operate. We've watched visionaries like Ralph Baxter who led Orrick, Herrington & Sutcliffe LLP for twenty-three years. In 2002, the firm made the then audacious move to take eighty of their employees, those involved in world-wide support service operations such as information technology, accounts receivable, and human resources, and centralize those services in Wheeling, West Virginia. By doing so, Baxter aimed to offer greater efficiency and cost reduction for the firm and its clients. In 2004, Baxter was followed by David Perla and Sanjay Kamlani who took the concept a step further: overseas. Their company Pangea3 moved legal operations an even greater distance by taking the concept of legal process outside of the typical law firm, allowing law firms and corporations to utilize the talents of their company's operations in India.

We've seen advances in other areas. For example, the country has seen women become more of a driving force in the law. Barbara Paul Robinson became the first female President of the New York City Bar Association; Roberta Cooper Ramo became the first female head of the American Bar Association; Regina Pisa became head of Goodwin Procter LLP; and Candace Beinecke led Hughes Hubbard & Reed LLP. All of this was set upon a stage where we finally saw women take their seats on the U.S. Supreme Court. The equal role of women in the law has become an accepted state, though much more needs to be accomplished on behalf of both women and minorities.

We've seen mega mergers of large law firms that create complex business models. These new organizations are both ripe with exciting opportunities for growth and innovation, and new challenges that may at times seem insurmountable.

8

And Yet, We Persist

In sum, the approach of law firms to marketing and business development — as well as the business of law generally — has certainly changed in the last few decades. But while some things have dramatically changed, others have not. At times it's still difficult to conclude exactly why a client hires a law firm: Is it strictly the relationship of the lawyer to the client, the security of the firm's brand in the boardroom, or which firm offers the best price or greatest value proposition? Often it's more than one factor. It's also still a challenge to convince some lawyers that marketing their professional skills is a good thing, not a bad one, and there remain some lawyers who approach overall marketing with distrust. Marketing has changed with the times from the days of the *Bates* decision, but the profession is still evolving.

In the rest of this book, I will explore the themes introduced above, and much more, to provide an overview of the various ways lawyers and law firms develop business. In order to provide the best view on what is happening today and to include ideas and tools with the greatest value for the future, I consulted with many leading marketers, law firm leaders, general counsel, consultants and other innovators — all incredible professionals. Each had a unique perspective on legal marketing, business development and/or legal operations. My aim with this book is to consolidate some of that thinking into one place, as a guide to lawyers managing the marketing function, marketers overseeing these changes, and the consultants who work advising the profession.

One thing I have learned throughout this process is that we still have a lot to learn from one another.

Chapter 2

Technology and Marketing:

The Impact of Procurement, Proposals, Outsourcing and AI

In the last few years, the legal profession has felt a seismic jolt: our own "lawland" equivalent of the Big Bang. Changes appear to be coming from all directions: from the economy, from our clients, but mostly in the form of new technology. Technology is impacting the way that most of us — whether we are vendors, marketers or practitioners — think about and manage legal work. The impact on how firms market themselves is driven by these changes. Just one indication is the creation of several new roles being developed at law firms; we now have officers of innovation, procurement specialists and pricing managers.

While there are many factors forcing this change, it appears that most reverberations are triggered by two factors: the desire of general counsel and their companies to control legal spend and therefore force change at the provider level, and the efficiencies enabled by emerging new technology. Still, the adoption of technology and adaptation to new expectations requires changes in behavior.

Think of the success of Uber, Via and Lyft. They represent the combination of a desire to get someplace quickly, in a relatively inexpensive way, paired with the availability of satellite technology. Look at Netflix and other streaming video services. There is a demand for curating our own television viewing habits, in much the way we've been able to create music playlists or accommodate our own reading habits. Now with technology, we can control where we watch, when we watch, and how much we watch, by pairing ourselves with streaming services that allow on-demand viewing.

With legal services, change is driven by the need to sync in-house counsel's demand for greater value, with the availability of new technologies and the advent of legal process outsourcing. Change is coming quickly.

Proposals and Auctions

As a law firm CMO, I always tracked patterns to see how business was being generated. When I saw repeat referral sources or determined which marketing technique had an impact or demonstrated a return on investment, a lightbulb went on. Many marketers join me in that excitement and find that it's equally interesting to see which partners continuously do the best at using methods that retain brand new clients.

So how do clients come to a large law firm? It's likely that they are brought in by the same methods that draw clients to other general practice and specialist firms. Often, firms are hired because of a recommendation or a referral. Other times, it is through a banker, accountant, or other intermediary who has gotten to know the firm by being on the other side of an engagement.

While lawyers often say a new client "came to me because of my reputation," reputation is a murky trigger to track. Reputation involves a set of circumstances that cause someone, because of the strength of a brand or awareness of the person's expertise, to decide to hire a specific lawyer.

Referrals also come through clients who make a move to a new company and bring in new counsel at their new organization. And, if a law firm treats its own lawyers and staff well, values them, and stays in touch with them after they've left the firm, alumni referrals to the law firm can become among the most valuable sources of clients and meaningful referrals.

Long a staple familiar to law firms working with the government sector, the last ten years have seen requests for proposals (RFPs) become the norm for larger or more complex assignments. We've seen within the last decade, large RFPs lead to formal competitions in which firms have the chance to present their capabilities, à la *Mad Men,* and the advertising business of the 1960s. Responding to RFPs typically requires input from several departments within a law firm, including marketing, finance, information technology, and often pricing professionals. For many firms, the process can be a big drain on their marketing resources. In addition to RFPs, there are intermittent requests for information (RFIs) that may come during an engagement, or to a firm from a long-term client.

The types of information that may be requested by an RFP include:

- Expertise: Representative cases or transactions
- Industry experience
- Proposed staffing
- Proposed fees/costs
- Cyber and other information security protocols
- Alternative/creative fee arrangements
- Geographic range
- Current business conflicts and processes for how they'll be handled in the future
- Diversity profile
- Technological capabilities
- Value-added activities
- Environmental impact

- References
- Corporate social responsibility

When an RFP is not part of the process, a new-business pitch package may still be required. While the responses crafted by law firms used to be heavily text-laden pieces, today we are more likely to see flip books or a one-pager, often referred to as a placemat, brought to a meeting.

And there is one type of pitch that strikes terror in the heart of most law firm marketers: the reverse auction, where an assignment will presumably go to one of if not the lowest bidders on a fixed-price matter. Think of it as eBay, but in reverse, for a preselected group of law firms. While each firm invited to pitch could presumably do the job, pricing is a big consideration and the metric upon which the competition is based.

Dan Troy, Senior Vice President & General Counsel of GlaxoSmithKline (GSK), received attention a few years ago for implementing an innovative reverse auction practice at the pharmaceutical giant. It wasn't simply that Dan triggered a movement of in-house counsel using technology to lower legal costs; it was that in 2013, the work served as the subject for a groundbreaking case study for Harvard Business School, "GlaxoSmithKline: Sourcing Complex Professional Services," conducted by Dr. Silvia Hodges Silverstein and Dr. Heidi K. Gardner.[1] The piece has been credited with helping initiate important conversations on the topic of procurement and collaboration among the legal marketing and legal operations and procurement communities.

Using a rigorous data-driven approach to hiring firms, GSK developed a system whereby it invites several firms that qualify for an engagement to bid for the business using an electronic bidding

---

1. Heidi K. Gardner and Silvia Hodges Silverstein, GlaxoSmithKline: Sourcing Complex Professional Services (Harvard Business Review Case Study 2013).

program. The bidding process takes a few hours, and requires that each firm has someone online providing their lowest bid against other firms in real time. The case study is a must read for anyone who wants to know more about the legal procurement process.

Dan's team at GSK is called GELRT, the Global External Legal Relations Team. GSK's policy is to send every representation over $100,000 through GELRT. Dan explains that the process is so successful and relatively easy to use that some in-house counsel at the company even want to use it for projects that come in below $100,000. Dan says, "The reverse auction set-up can be accomplished in two days. It's an investment, but it pays off in money and time. It's what many of us call our electronic sourcing room."

"You need to understand that not everyone can be Wachtell in every practice area. Instead, firms should be able to articulate that they are great at these one, two or three things."

—Daniel Troy, GlaxoSmithKline

When Dan started his law firm career at Sidley Austin, he was handling a client matter that required FDA approval. It was work that his client urgently needed done in a very short time frame. Through a combination of Dan's know-how and tenacity on the matter, he was able to get the approval granted weeks before the client's deadline. The client was surprised and delighted. A few months later, another client was facing a tough problem that was likely to trigger a huge stock price drop for the company, but because Dan was able to find an innovative solution to the client's problem, the crisis was averted. The company held onto millions of dollars worth of stock value that it would have otherwise lost. The problem was mitigated by the speedy nature of the resolution.

In both instances, Dan was more efficient than the billable hour being charged would have reflected; instead, he solved the client's problem within his own time frame.

"The billable hour doesn't align with the proper incentives," says Dan. "Law firms have an ethical duty to represent clients with 'zealous advocacy.' Yet, the billable hour pits client versus law firm and creates a financial conflict of interest from the very beginning of the engagement. Flat fees and success fees align all interests to ensure we are all pulling in the same direction — the best interests of the client whereby the lawyer has an incentive to win and will aim for early resolution."

Beyond price, Dan points out that there is a huge issue of credibility when selecting a law firm. His advice to law firms is that they can't survive on a model of being all things to all people. "Clients' mindsets have changed," says Dan. "The day of giving all your work to one law firm as opposed to the best in each practice is over."

Trying to be all things to all people is no longer the way to practice law. The firms that are best positioned for success have learned to focus their efforts. Dan says, "You need to understand that not everyone can be Wachtell in every practice area. Instead, firms should be able to articulate that they are great at these one, two or three things."

As it is a brave new world, law firms are more open to offering alternative fees. Dan says that there are several firms that will work with him on this basis. It has been a success on both sides. He points out that these are firms that generally take more of a long view to growing their business, rather than looking solely at short-term gains.[2]

---

2.   *Id.*

There are two new disciplines within corporations that are helping GCs like Dan as they professionalize the operations of in-house legal departments: Procurement and Operations.

Procurement

The concept of procurement services has been around for a long time. Procurement first came to the architectural and engineering professions, then to the creative services, such as marketing and PR agencies. In more recent years, the impact has been felt by accounting and auditing firms. It's only a relatively recent development that procurement services have been used by corporate legal departments.

Using a procurement process, a legal department can develop a short list of law firms it wants to consider for an assignment or category of assignments. The firms then put together the best pricing packages they can, and the legal department or a procurement professional makes a recommendation of the best firms out of those, based on the cost of the assignment and its value.

In 2014, Silvia Hodges Silverstein, the co-author of the Harvard Business School case study on GSK's reverse auction system, launched the Buying Legal Council, the international trade organization for the legal procurement profession. Today, the organization has more than 650 members and affiliated friends around the world. The goal of the group is to facilitate a dialogue between buyers and sellers of legal services. Most legal procurement professionals report to a Chief Procurement Officer and many of them are not lawyers, but they may have a BA in Finance or an MBA.

According to Yolanda Cartusciello, a partner at the consulting firm PP&C Consulting, LLC, the emergence of the procurement professional is actually an opportunity for marketing professionals. Yolanda contends, "Smart law firm marketers should be able to reach out and develop good relationships with these professionals. To the CMOs, I would say, 'How often do you have contacts on the client side who can tell you what they are thinking?' If you think about it, it's a golden opportunity and of course they will speak with you. Their jobs are predicated on how to save their companies money. They are more than happy to pinpoint the pain points."

And there will be even more of an opportunity to reach out and grow relationships with procurement officers. The worst thing a law firm can do is ignore procurement. You want to know how these professionals approach controlling costs, how they measure success, and how they themselves are evaluated. According to Silvia, "It's not just the financial savings, but help in projecting the legal spend and making it more predictable. They've baked it into the process so that they can make the legal process more predictable."

Legal Operations

With the growth of the in-house legal department, there is a recognized need for efficiency within the general counsel's office, not just at the outside law firms. While pricing will always be a key component of operating a legal department, improving its operations is the name of the game. By the mid-1980s, many companies increasingly handled a broad set of legal matters in-house. While corporations still used outside counsel, in-house legal teams grew not only in the scope of matters they addressed but also in terms of total legal professional headcount. By 2000, technology companies started to offer a broader set of increasingly better solutions to address everything from e-billing and matter management to e-discovery, automated workflows, data analytics and more. And finally, around the same time, alternative legal service providers started to come into their own, providing legal support at lower costs and equal or better quality than law firms. In combination, these factors gave rise to legal operations roles — individuals dedicated to optimizing in-house legal support at the lowest cost possible. By 2010, many large and medium-sized companies had small operations teams, but the function was still not clearly defined and there was no reference model for performing legal operations.

To bring greater order to the operations space, operations professionals started forming small groups to discuss best practices. One of these groups was founded in 2010 by Connie Brenton of Oracle's legal department. It was particularly successful and grew to include more than forty companies on the West Coast. Struggling to keep up with member growth and seeing an opportunity to do so much more than just share best practices, in 2016, Connie (who by then had moved to NetApp, Inc.) and eight others founded the Corporate Legal Operations Consortium (CLOC). Six of the eight founders are current Board of Directors and Leadership Members: Jeffrey Franke (Yahoo, Inc.); Mary Shen O'Carroll (Google LLC); Christine Coats (Oracle Corporation); Steven Harmon (Cisco Systems, Inc.); Brian Hupp (Facebook, Inc.) and Lisa Konie (Adobe Systems Inc.). CLOC grew quickly, and the organization now represents more than 800 companies, including more than 30% of the Fortune 500, in forty countries, representing more than $40 billion in annual legal spend.

Connie explains, "What a chief of staff or legal operations person does, in essence, is an amalgamation of the administrative side of a law firm. We're responsible for twelve core competencies, including the financial matters such as budgeting and managing spend among legal department teams; outside counsel engagement; technology implementation; team development, organizational design, and team member development; data analytics and much more. It's a huge role. Prior to CLOC's existence, there was no definition. And part of what we've done over time is help define and lay these things out and then provide training, best practices, templates, benchmarking and more. And that is what CLOC is all about. Really refining what that is."

While each day is different in the role of an operations professional, the one thing that remains the same is the frenetic pace of managing a complex organization. "A day in the life of an operations professional involves dealing with the burning fires that come up on any number of the twelve core competencies, everything from electronic billing matters to technology implementations," says Connie. The role can involve everything from meeting with third-party providers to develop legal coverage models to working closely with law firms to creating knowledge management solutions. "We identify which firms are really killing it," says Connie, "and which firms we might need to reach out to because maybe they have a problem with us, or alternatively, they're not delivering against expectations."

Legal Process Outsourcing

When I asked Dan Troy about the idea of outsourcing routine work to a lower cost provider, he had an interesting take on things. He believes that the first step is to create a great process internally, then look at outside resources. "Why not consider taking an internal team that takes standardized contracts and put them into one place within the organization?" he asks.

That is exactly what Dan has done in a number of cases. He believes law firms should do the same by disaggregating the way they do their work and in particular, look at things like e-discovery and document teams. Then consider if they really want to be doing this type of work or if they can do it in a less expensive cost structure.

Two leaders in law firm technology and legal process outsourcing (LPOs) are David Perla and Sanjay Kamlani, who together in 2004 founded Pangea3. Pangea3 grew to become one of the largest LPO companies in the world, and in 2010, was acquired by Thomson Reuters. Pangea3 clients include leading law firms and corporations, such as GE, Credit Suisse, United Technologies, Sony, American Express, Philip Morris, and Deutsche Bank. David and Sanjay agree that there is an opportunity for LPO any time a firm is doing something operational, or anything that is highly repeatable and can be reduced to a process, with any sort of regularity. They note that there are many different approaches to handling this work. They cite that WilmerHale has its operations in Dayton and Orrick has its operations in West Virginia. "Some firms see this as a plus for their clients and publicly laud the merits of handling this work, off premise, while others shy away from talking about it," says David.

Bob Rowe is the CEO of Integreon, Inc., a global provider of legal processing work and one of a handful of companies that expanded over the past decade to manage the discovery process for law firms, store data, and handle other administrative and business services for firms. He says, "If you need a great litigator and have a specific legal problem, David Boies will take care of bespoke problems, but when you have tens of thousands of generally repetitive NDAs for drafting and filing, it makes little sense to pay premium rates for such high-volume, lower-risk activities. What is required is a scalable process, which alternative legal service providers like ours are better suited to handle."

"I do think the data explosion is getting worse and worse," he continued. "E-discovery started and every year people say the amount of data is doubling and tripling. The increasing volume has outstripped many pricing models, requiring service providers to constantly innovate to increase scalability, lower prices and continue to make E-discovery services affordable."

But not everyone feels the need to change. Bob points out that law firms are losing speed, in part because of their reluctance to invest in innovation. "It's often entities other than law firms that bring the innovation," says Bob. "Just look at the launch of the law firm ILC Legal by the accounting firm PwC. Given the growth of alternative legal service providers, general counsel wield more power than ever before and it is a buyer's market."

It seems that clients want to pay for analysis but not the unnessary process behind the analysis. According to those I spoke with in the legal process area, quite often it's the client who calls and points out that the firm is doing something repetitive.

"For a significant merger, there are hundreds of thousands of contracts that must be analyzed and organized. Software and the use of technology as part of a scalable process really is the only way to attack this challenge," says Bob.

And if the flat fee that we hear about makes sense, why wouldn't lawyers want to make the process as efficient as possible?

Artificial Intelligence

There are three value propositions that David Perla and Sanjay Kamlani tell me to remember: cheaper, better, faster. "Will a new process do this? Will AI accomplish this? Is it faster and can it be deployed in a practical way? Better? Not sure. Cheaper? Again, not sure. So the results need to be better. The problems are still there," says David.

According to David, from what he sees in the law firm space, most of the AI being used could be considered a "bolt-on," and just one more application that doesn't connect with the others. This is a problem about which to be wary.

Mark T. Greene, a consultant in the innovation space, believes that law firms should proceed cautiously. "Firms should start with their agreed upon business needs and then consider whether an AI tool might be part of the solution for that need. Too many begin by deciding that they 'want to try AI' before they have identified the need to which it will be applied. Generally, AI solutions will not be standalone systems, but instead must be integrated with the firm's other systems, such as billing, CRM and external vendors such as LexisNexis and Thomson Reuters," he says.

"Some AI tools are clearly delivering on the promise of better, faster, cheaper. These began with eDiscovery, and then contracts. Legal research tools are also being successfully deployed by some firms." Greene continues, "I post on my blog examples of this success almost every day. Other AI systems, such as predictive analytics, are still in their infancy and somewhat hit or miss."

"These successful AI tools are not limited to the practice of law; they assist with the business of law as well. While the legal industry generally lags behind the Big Four accounting firms in terms of deploying such tools, in the most progressive firms AI can be found in finance, HR, and marketing departments. 'Predictive pitching' is especially intriguing as AI will allow efficient processing of hundreds of variables across thousands of matters to identify the predictors of various sorts of legal needs before clients know they are in need of counsel," he said.

What will create adoption of the new technologies? It used to be that law firms had supply and clients had demand, but now it's completely changed. Legal departments are in the driver's seat and there is a confluence of events that are forcing change.

Michael Mills is the Co-Founder and Chief Strategy Officer of Neota Logic Inc. and an expert in the AI area. His company refers to itself as a provider of an AI-driven platform for intelligent automation of expertise, documents, and processes. Michael was formerly a partner at Mayer Brown LLP and subsequently joined Davis Polk & Wardwell LLP as its first Chief Knowledge Officer.

I asked Michael about the fact that for many years, technology-assisted review (TAR), had been used to analyze gigantic data sets of e-discovery. Why now is AI growing? According to Michael, four factors are driving the growth of AI across all industries: (1) data in computable form, unfathomable oceans of it; (2) computing in the cloud, on-demand access to effectively unlimited power; (3) improved algorithms, building on neural network models originally conceived in the 1980s; and (4) algorithms-as-a-service, provided by the big players (Amazon, Facebook, Google, IBM, Microsoft) on demand to any company, large or small.

Michael points out that there are two other factors that apply to law. "Client demands for 'more for less,' have risen steadily since 2008. Even the fanciest firms doing the highest value work are expected to be efficient. Also, it's key to keep in mind that dozens of specialist software companies have been launched to apply AI tools and techniques to legal services, as is also happening in financial services and marketing," he says.

The science is fundamentally not new according to Michael. "What's new is the engineering — the ability to select and tune good algorithms and run them at vast scale. Amazon, Facebook, etc., are not using AI to be more efficient; they are using AI to create new services. Law, however, is using AI to be more efficient."

Michael and others believe that even those firms that are unsure about new technology should open the door to vendors who will be knocking. "Don't waste time or buy a lot, but do coax lawyers to sit through one-hour demonstrations several times a year," he says.

Over the long term we must assume there will be significant effects from this technology, even if we don't know yet what they look like. When AI is progressing so rapidly in so many areas, why would law be immune? Michael says, "In the near term, the impact will be material, that is, affect law firm revenue in only two areas: the first is e-discovery, where adoption of AI techniques under the label TAR is still surprisingly low, less than one-third of cases, and the second is due diligence document review, which is a task quite similar to e-discovery. However, even in e-discovery, firms can still tout their competence with TAR because so many other firms still drag their heels and don't train partners, or even associates, in the tools and methods."

Michael and others warn firms that receive substantial revenue from lawyers doing the tasks that can be helped by automation to plan for loss of that revenue in the next couple of years.

David Perla and Sanjay Kamlani observe that many of the larger law firms are putting together innovation committees or hiring a Chief Innovation Officer to figure out how to best use technologies. Without internal innovation committees or partners in charge of innovation, many firms try on various tools, like pieces of clothing, just to see what works within a specific practice. They do not think through the overall integration or implementation.

"Firms need to understand how they are going to incorporate innovations and tools in their processes and how the economics work if processes are going to change and impact costs and billing," says Sanjay. If a firm is using it for existing fixed-fee projects, it is easier to see how it is going to work. However, "If you are talking about real artificial intelligence, or machine learning, you need to know where you are headed," he advises.

Marketers and Innovation

Bill Carter is the Chief Executive Officer of ALM, the information and media company that publishes the *American Lawyer* and many other trade publications. He is known as one of the most innovative people in publishing. Bill says, "Legal marketers need to adapt to a new pace of innovation driven by changing client expectations. Building a personal relationship between lawyer and client will remain important, but it is not enough. Clients increasingly expect a broader and deeper relationship with both the lawyer and firm. In response, the most innovative legal marketers will experiment and borrow tactics utilized by other B2B companies."

Outsourcing and standardized work will also have an impact, and there is great potential for the two concepts to work together. According to Bill, "Outsourcing has arrived in the largest corporate legal departments. The cost savings from DXC and GE's outsourcing to UnitedLex are too meaningful to ignore. Others will follow." It appears that by being data driven, companies like UnitedLex will be able to measure even more results and outcomes ever more closely.

Bill is also interested in looking at all forms of artificial technology, and how it might be applied, even in today's world. "Chatbots may be in our future, with simple conversations and answers to simplistic legal questions. Can you imagine questions about immigration law being answered in a simple way and even helping to produce a document to file? It's out there today." Bill says, "AI and other emerging technologies have the potential to improve and enhance customer service."

One of the firms best known for innovation is the global firm Allen & Overy LLP. According to Lee Garfinkle, Chief Marketing and Business Development Officer of the Americas, for many years, the firm has taken a holistic view on the delivery of legal services and meeting client needs. Allen & Overy's Advanced Delivery platform was established to develop innovative solutions through the use of people, processes, and technology.

LAW FIRM BUSINESS DEVELOPMENT AND MARKETING

One recent output of this platform was a system called MarginMatrix™. New regulations took effect in 2016 which required every major bank in the world to design and negotiate new and complex documentation — often with more than 10,000 counterparties — in order to implement new margin rules. MarginMatrix™ essentially codified the laws in various jurisdictions and automated the drafting of tailored documents based on an automated legal analysis. Allen & Overy then collaborated with Deloitte to deliver an end-to-end solution for this challenge to clients.

But what do practicing lawyers and law firm leaders think about innovation? Charles Martin, a highly respected law firm leader and Senior Partner with Macfarlanes LLP in the UK, comments, "Innovation means two things that are interrelated, but essentially different. One is that it is about doing the same tasks more efficiently and therefore creating greater efficiency. Some of the benefit, but not the entirety of it, is usually passed onto the client. It allows clients to use a more premium firm at a lower but still high cost or to use the same firm that they would otherwise use but pay less for it. More for less is the mantra of the times. And this is the holy grail, clearly, of many corporate counsel. So, efficiency is one side of innovation."

Charles continues, "But, another side is doing a better job: it is also about quality. Some of the tools provide a combination of robots, AI, and big data, and give clients all kinds of benefits. For example, a better and more accurate assessment of liability issues where you are not just saying, 'Well in my experience…,' but you are actually able to back it up with a hard assessment of the risk. That has a long way to go but it's quite exciting and very valuable."

Conclusion

The plethora of alternatives to the hiring of a traditional law firm is growing, most notably legal process outsourcing providers and accounting firms that are entering into the legal landscape. Add to this the possibilities of legal work being produced and delivered to a client through the impact of better technologies, greater project management and resources made possible by artificial intelligence and machine learning.

The potential of all of these occurrences could be good, bad, terrifying or all three — at the same time. Still, they offer great potential to lawyers and legal marketers who strive to be ahead of the curve. Like any change in business, opportunities often go to those who move first.

Think Piece

Evolution Through Adaptation

By Sanjay Kamlani and David Perla*

In June 2017, we wrote an article, "Power to the People," in which we offered that technology would enable rather than replace legal professionals. We argued that while legal jobs would change, technology would open more doors than it would close, and that professionals embracing technology would have many new opportunities at their fingertips. We continue to hold that view. But after spending the last year reviewing countless new legaltech offerings, and advising a wide range of organizations on legaltech and legal innovation, our strong sense is that innovation and transformation is going to be accomplished more by those who can change behavior than by those who offer the best or most impactful technology.

Recently, our industry has seen a marked increase in "savior" technology, with newer saviors appearing more rapidly over time. From legal outsourcing (our origins as entrepreneurs), to full-service alternative legal service providers, to analytics (litigation and contract), artificial intelligence, blockchain and smart contracts, law is inundated with both rapidly released technologies and a never-ending stream of press about the changes these new tech-

---

*   Sanjay Kamlani is Managing Director at 1991 Group, where he advises clients on legal technology and services, outsourcing and cross-border business issues. David Perla is Managing Director at Burford Capital, responsible for overseeing Burford's global origination and marketing efforts, and is based in New York. Entrepreneurs and legal industry leaders with expertise in building high-growth legal and technology-driven businesses, Sanjay and David are the Co-Founders and former Co-CEOs of Pangea3, the legal outsourcing company acquired by Thomson Reuters. Sanjay and David were each named a Top 50 Innovator of the Last 50 Years by the *American Lawyer*.

nologies will bring. New entrants appear faster, release products sooner, and copy one another quicker than ever before. Despite all that, and the nearly ubiquitous press coverage of it, change remains incremental and measured, both at law firms and at clients. Why? And what can entrepreneurs do about it?

Darwin is often inaccurately quoted as saying "It is not the strongest of the species that survives, nor the most intelligent that survives. It is the one that is most adaptable to change." Notwithstanding that Darwin never actually said these words, the principle espoused is widely accepted — namely, that change comes from adaptation, not strength. We submit that in the legal industry, change will be driven not by those with the best products or technology, nor even by those that offer solutions that allow clients to be the most efficient or most effective. Rather, change will be driven by those companies and entrepreneurs that are most capable of facilitating incremental adaptation within their clients, and between their clients and their client's clients and vendors.

In our practice, we meet regularly with companies, law firms and legal departments, and solutions providers. In speaking with prospective clients of new legal technologies, we see a sincere desire to explore new technologies, to become more efficient and to serve end-clients more efficiently and more effectively. Our clients recognize that the world is changing quickly and embrace the need to adopt new methods of getting their work done, and of creating and selling their products. That said, the legal industry is an old one, with ingrained habits, many of which have protected and benefitted clients for decades, and even centuries. Many of those habits are themselves the product of prior innovations from prior disruptive waves — disruptions both specifically focused on lawyers (e.g., electronic research replacing books) and more broadly focused disruptions (e.g., Google wasn't created for lawyers, but nearly all young lawyers now embrace Google during their legal research and analysis, along with other tools). The major difference we see today is that today's innovators want to create massive change quickly, and often assume that the technology or product alone can do that.

This is a fallacy, and frustrates entrepreneurs, investors and clients alike.

In our view, creating the change so many of us seek in the industry requires creating a structure that enables, encourages and rewards adaptation at the client, and at its ultimate client and vendors, and does so in a way that is impactful, but not intrusive or condescending. We observe a wide variety of vendor practices, few of which find the necessary balance between offering impactful, accurate technology on the one hand, and a system that encourages broad-based behavior change on the other hand, even when that behavior change is expressly desired by the client.

Take contract authoring tools — like the more mature and antiquated HotDocs, and more recent Contract Express and more entrepreneurial Leaflet, for example — tools that enable document forms (e.g., sales contract form, deportation waiver application, motion to dismiss pleading) to be linked to a questionnaire such that an attorney can create a new document specific to a new matter simply by answering the questionnaire from which the software automatically edits the document. Attorneys report significant time savings from drafting documents without the tool (i.e., the traditional method of pulling the document from the last matter and redlining it based on the facts of the new matter). The challenge is that one has to spend time learning how to use the software and, once mastered, it can still take twenty to fifty-plus hours to build a new form depending on complexity. And then there is the question about incentives — what is the benefit of saving time for an hourly billing lawyer? These products require real behavior change, significant time investment and a change in the incentives around contract drafting. So the months of effort that go into the sales cycle (from the vendor's perspective) and the selection process (from the client's perspective) are just the pre-game event. Once purchased, the vendor and buyer often don't even show up to the game. They simply add the software to the law client's tools platform, add it to the multiple screen list of products on an already-crowded portal, and announce several software launch training sessions which are sparsely attended — often for lack of an incentive to attend. The result: few users and even less long-term adoption. But when providers build a full-fledged training and service program around the tool and consult with clients about best practices and how they can build a program to incentivize lawyer use, the product sticks and adoption starts to take hold.

Ultimately, this technology, like others, will achieve an accelerating rate of adoption with one to three market leading providers and a sense of ubiquity. Relativity has achieved this in the e-discovery space, and Practical Law in the online learning and practical guidance space, but only after a decade-plus-long evolutionary process of adoption. On the other hand, with technology that is just loaded onto client platforms and simply made available for lawyers to choose to use, the likelihood is that those technologies will die young.

We remain optimistic that positive change is afoot in the legal industry. But we are cautious about the rate of that change, and about which companies and products will ultimately prevail. For those entrepreneurs and companies with innovative solutions, and all of those seeking to drive the change we all seek, we encourage more effort at holistic solutions that bring about not merely great products, but also programmatic and incremental adaptations on the client side. This will require more effort at the client, more time listening, and more time and resources devoted to teaching, aiding, and incentivizing clients in their journey toward more tech-driven and efficient solutions for their end-user clients.

Chapter 3

Client Relations

How do lawyers create long-term relationships with clients — those seemingly mythical engagements that go on for years? We've all heard of such relationships, where the client turns to the lawyer to handle his or her most important legal matters as well as to receive other commercial advice. It's where the client becomes an apostle, singing the praises of the lawyer to others without ever being asked to do so. The truth is that these relationships are not a myth. Even today, in a world of procurement, RFPs and heightened competition, they do exist.

If you ask a room of legal rainmakers how they maintain loyal clients who have grown into long-term engagements, you will get a host of different answers. Of course, there are some common behaviors, including providing outstanding client service, viewing the engagement through the client's eyes, and digging in to understand the industry practices. The tactics the rainmakers employ, however, are widespread and varied. Here are some insights.

The Rainmaker's Perspective

Traditionally, the client service partner is the partner who nurtures the relationship and helps it to grow. While coaching can certainly help improve skills in this area, role modeling has also proven to be useful. Understanding the tools and skills that others have successfully used may be the first great step in the right direction.

Jeffrey S. Klein, Head of Weil, Gotshal & Manges LLP's Employment Litigation practice and a management-side counselor, excels at client care. Jeff is a great listener but also has an innate ability to anticipate the needs of his clients. He genuinely cares about his clients and looks out for their best long-term interests.

Jeff's services are always in demand. There is a constant flow of CEOs, General Counsel, HR executives, and professional athletes coming to his office. How is it that he learned to develop new business? Was it trial and error, or is it in his DNA?

Jeff doesn't believe that there is a business development gene but rather a business development muscle that someone can build over time. Making an analogy to athletics, Jeff offers two points to consider: "First, very few people can start a workout program being able to bench press 200 pounds or run a marathon. Second, just as there are many different sports, there are many different ways to develop business, and someone who is talented at baseball may not be very good at figure skating, and vice versa. Thus, a thorough evaluation of one's strengths and weaknesses is critical to effectively and correctly apply the business development muscle, and practice and training is necessary to improve and tone it."

Lawyers who want to grow their practice have the opportunity to demonstrate their skill by moderating panels and speaking at conferences, writing articles, attending and networking at bar association events, presenting client CLE's, participating in shared community service or pro bono activities, and engaging in one-on-one socializing. Jeff believes that by participating in a variety of activities, soon enough, you get stronger at identifying those that work for you. The activities that work for you — if you do them often enough — become muscle memory.

Jeff says, "For me, it was a combination of matching the business development activities with my skill set, and then focusing on practice and repetition."

Mentorship and the ability to learn from strong leadership can make all of the difference to a developing lawyer. Jeff notes, "Like many fine Weil attorneys before me, I would certainly thank Ira Millstein, one of the founding fathers of our firm. Ira's approach was collaborative and designed to engender confidence in his partners. He would make an introduction to a client, and then let you — in fact, expected you to — run things as you saw fit and in accordance with your strengths. Indeed, his view was that any business that you could bring in was a great learning experience in business development and client management."

Jeff recalls a time when he had an opportunity to bring in a new client: Al Leiter, a rookie baseball player who was thought to be the New York Yankees' next star pitcher. This took place at a time when Jeff already represented another baseball player, Dave Winfield. "I was mocked by some of my other partners for trying to represent athletes and grow a practice from the ground up. But Ira promised to support me in pursuing this type of practice, and he did," says Jeff.

Jeff has become good friends with many of his clients, whether athletes or business leaders. "Especially in my line of business, which involves sensitive and critical company issues that often require resolution in the midst of a crisis, you tend to get to know people on a personal level. And you tend to try to alleviate the pressure of the day by delving into non-substantive topics when there is a break," he says.

But Jeff also attributes his success to his adopting of a long view toward client relationships. "A lesson that I learned a long time ago was to cultivate relationships with the entire client team, not just the General Counsel or most senior in-house lawyer," says Jeff. "Junior lawyers grow up in an organization, and I made it a point to regularly check in on them when I visited the company's headquarters. Several remarked to me years later, when they were responsible for selection and hiring of outside counsel, that they remembered those conversations in detail."

David Bernstein, Chair of Debevoise's Intellectual Property Litigation Group, has a talent for making each of his clients feel like they are his only client. David was inspired by his father, who was a rainmaker on Wall Street and the consummate salesman. "I grew up watching him identify, attract, entertain, and care about clients. He took them to dinner. He golfed with them. He invited them on trips. He played tennis with them, and took them skiing, and even included them on our family vacations. Everything revolved around his clients," says David.

David watched his father with awe because the elder Bernstein was so extroverted. "He would walk up to strangers in restaurants and strike up conversations. He talked to people sitting next to him at Rangers games. He exchanged cards with prospective clients on the ski chairlift," says David. And though it seemed aggressive at the time to David, it almost always resulted in a conversation, and usually developed into a new client.

David, in contrast, was initially more of an introvert. "I forced myself to do the same. It was hard at first — walking up to strangers at legal conferences or cocktail parties — but it became easier over time since it never resulted in the embarrassment or disaster that I feared. And as it become less awkward I learned that it actually was fun," he says.

David's clients too often become friends. "Making friends with my clients is easy. First of all, our firm's clients are incredible people. They are smart, ambitious, and running great businesses. They also are all in a time of crisis, needing the expert assistance that we can bring to bear. And we respond as friends — devoting all of our time, energy and resources to solving their problems," he says. "We work side-by-side, shoulder-to-shoulder, strategizing about the issues, understanding the problem, and devising solutions. It is an intimate experience and hardly a surprise that it leads to deep connections."

David makes a strong effort to stay in touch with clients, even if he has no further business with them. "Clients are human. Celebrate the momentous events in their lives. Clients also are interested in other opportunities, and I regularly share new in-house opportunities with my clients when I think there might be a promising fit."

Charles Martin of Macfarlanes remarks that the way for a lawyer to remain competitive and develop clients is to serve as a client's trusted advisor. Charles also believes that it is critical to have bulletproof and rigorous independence. That requires intellectual credibility and an ability to add tangible value as well. Independence, fairness, objectivity, and experience are essential. But Charles points out, "years and years of experience allow you to bring a perspective to bear, beyond technical credentials, that clients really value and might not get from anywhere else."

"You need to be the person who can inspire confidence and absolute, unquestionable confidentiality. And inspiring confidence is partly about unlearning some of what you may have learned at law school: being able to listen and challenge in a constructive way. That is a talent that you can't fake. It means that you need to be a nuanced and refined listener, establishing rapport and demonstrating a propensity for emotional intelligence. Traditional legal training does not necessarily arm you with these skills because it's nearly always about the transmit and being the smartest transmitter in the room," says Charles.

Pierre Gentin was Managing Director and Global Head of Litigation and Regulatory Investigations at Credit Suisse during the 2008 financial crisis. Now a partner at Cahill Gordon & Reindel LLP, he applies his knowledge to working on the other side of the coin as a legal provider.

Pierre's experience as a client for nearly twenty years has impacted his approach working as outside counsel. In his experience, clients value lawyers who are analytically strong, hard-working and responsive, and who are willing — in a diplomatic and respectful way — to provide honest assessments, creative strategies, and robust, balanced advocacy.

Pierre says, "The issue of law firm cost is critical but doesn't exist in a vacuum. The healthiest professional relationship is one in which the in-house lawyer is truly confident that the outside counsel is doing all they can, with quality and integrity, to meet various important needs of the client. Those include general professional excellence, reliability and responsiveness, creative solutions and strong substantive outcomes, willingness to move mountains for the client, and a demonstrated ability to work aggressively with the client, as a part of that overall relationship, to respect the client's critical goals regarding cost."

"The issue of law firm cost is critical but doesn't exist in a vacuum. The healthiest professional relationship is one in which the in-house lawyer is truly confident that the outside counsel is doing all they can, with quality and integrity, to meet various important needs of the client."

—Pierre M. Gentin, Cahill Gordon & Reindel LLP

Securities litigator Ralph Ferrara, who was the youngest lawyer to ever serve as General Counsel of the SEC, started in private practice ten years after many of his contemporaries. He is now a partner at Proskauer Rose LLP.

Ralph notes, "When I joined the law firm world, the model for a premier lawyer was a polymath model. If you characterized yourself as a specialist, you were looked at as a mechanic. Today, clients want to see core competency and substantive legal expertise in particular areas, so that a lawyer can quickly and efficiently get to the root of their problem."

Clients who seek Ralph's services are often in the midst of a crisis — the general counsel who has received a Wells notice[1] from

---

1.   A Wells Notice is a letter sent by the Securities and Exchange Commission stating that it may bring an enforcement action against the recipient.

the SEC, or a board member who suspects corporate malfeasance, for example. How does Ralph engender trust among his clients, particularly when they are in a precarious frame of mind and facing unknown circumstances? He says, "You have to show complete commitment to the client's cause."

Many of Ralph's clients return to him after they have moved to a new company and find themselves in need of his services. Other than those serial clients, how does he get new clients? "I'm not someone who goes out and does a lot of client entertaining," says Ralph. "I've never done that. I don't try to woo them. My reputation comes from the knowledge that I am there to do whatever it takes to protect my clients as well as their employees."

Barry Wolf is a private equity lawyer and the Executive Partner and Chair of the management committee of Weil, Gotshal & Manges. He is also on the board of several organizations including Weill Cornell Medical College and The Global Foundation for Eating Disorders. Barry, who has a reputation as an expert rainmaker, believes that having a "wow factor" is critical to winning new business. He says, "Lawyers need to do such a good job with whomever they work that the person says, 'Wow, what a great lawyer and what a great firm.' I believe that is the key to our developing business."

Barry learned about the wow factor, much like Jeff Klein, by observing Ira Millstein and others, including the late corporate bankruptcy leader, Harvey Miller. Barry says that by merely watching them one could tell that they were phenomenal lawyers.

Barry believes that the wow factor is a combination of excellent judgment, service, great creativity and problem solving. But how does Barry know that the wow factor works? "I've gotten more work from referrals than anything else, both from my existing clients and from the other side of the table. You still need to do some entertaining and networking, but most of my business generation has come through clients and others who have seen my work in a transaction. In fact, I recently got an engagement from someone who is a friend," said Barry. "He heard from a mutual acquaintance to contact me. My friend, of course, then says, 'why didn't you ever try to sell me?'"

Barry understands that there is a need to continually reinforce the strength of great work. People pay a high price for the services of a law firm like Weil so the services they deliver require they meet the highest levels of excellence. Barry mentions the wow factor in every speech he gives at the firm and makes sure that it is a consistent message. "I sometimes worry that younger partners may look at other aspects of networking and socializing and lose sight of what I think is the most important, that excellence. While we should all do pro bono and philanthropic work, and that may at times bring connections or business, unless you do excellent work for your clients, the other things won't matter."

The Value Proposition

I tend to think of the value proposition as the "why buy" approach to hiring a lawyer or law firm. What is it that makes the firm or the individual unique and why should a client hire them? The American Bar Association reports that in 2018, the United States had more than 1.3 million practicing lawyers.[2] With such a crowded market, how can one firm or one lawyer stand out? Why one firm, or why one lawyer, over another?

According to Barry, "For the market segment we are in, the value proposition we are selling is based on the talent and teamwork of our people and the fact that we are able to provide a better quality of service." Value in terms of handling a client's most important litigation and transactions means providing top service, excellent judgment, and an unmatched understanding of the market.

---

2. ABA National Lawyer Population Survey Historical Trend in Total National Lawyer Population 1878–2018, https://www.americanbar.org/content/dam/aba/administrative/market_research/Total_National_Lawyer_Population_1878-2018.authcheckdam.pdf.

Barry speaks of one M&A partner who reads every public company merger agreement of every transaction; he reads every single one to know what the terms are, and he does this in his spare time. It takes a lot of time, but that's dedication. And when he goes into a meeting, he can demonstrate his mastery of every important detail, for example, that in a particular transaction the reverse breakup fee was "x" dollars, or that they had "y" type of provision.

Barry points out that the market is paying for your legal knowledge and your understanding of the market. "Great lawyers need to consistently hone that ability," he says.

Pierre points out that the strongest value proposition for him to offer an in-house lawyer is that he has been in their shoes. "The role of a general counsel or senior in-house lawyer is not always well understood among outside counsel. The truth is that some of the most nuanced and sensitive legal work, as well as very difficult judgment calls, are frequently done internally in a company before outside counsel get involved." Having been on both sides of this equation, Pierre intrinsically understands the issue.

Ralph Ferrara says that the greatest value he brings to a matter is that he doesn't look at problems idiosyncratically. "Some lawyers may get very focused on the issue exactly in the way that the client initially presents it. I always approach every new matter in a holistic way. If a client comes to me with a class action on a motion to dismiss, I need to think about the problem and think of it as a Calder mobile. If you pull on one string, the whole thing will shift. You need to be concerned not just about the class action, but the white collar issues, shareholder derivative action, board issues and D&O insurance problems. All of these things could be collateral of the problem."

Jeff Klein explains how his clients perceive his value proposition. "I am a management-side employment litigator," says Jeff. "In 99% of my engagements, the person or people on the other side of the table from my client feel personally wronged and, as a result, may be less likely to make a decision regarding the path forward based solely on rational and objective criteria. My value proposition, or so I have been told by clients, is that from the outset I have a strategy plotted to the end result, and work to steer the matter in that direction as expeditiously as possible. In so doing, I look to develop a way to relate to my adversary and his/her client by being an active listener, trying to understand what is important to them, and establishing bona fide credibility by my actions that I can leverage at critical moments."

Another aspect of the value proposition Jeff finds helpful is something learned many years ago from Weil senior partner Carl Lobell — make the client your friend. Echoing the remarks of David Bernstein, Jeff understands that practicing law is, after all, a people business and legal skills are somewhat fungible. "Key to this philosophy is the genuineness of your overtures. If you say, 'Let me know if I can help you,' then you better mean it. I regularly use my network of friends to help clients, whether it be to source a new position, obtain medical care for a family member, or provide advice and guidance for one of their children," says Jeff.

David also points out, "Too often, clients focus only on hourly rates, and compare firms based on their rates. That is the wrong comparison: rather, it should be the value that each firm can deliver. Value has a number of components. One is the total cost of the matter. That is not always easy to predict in the context of a litigation, but we can help manage that by treating every decision that impacts cost as if it was our own money. So we staff matters leanly and pursue projects that make economic sense," says David. "But value is also about the outcome of the matter. We care deeply about success because our client's success is our success, and we are, therefore, increasingly developing alternative fee arrangements that take success into account. Successful AFAs have to work for both the client and the law firm — they cannot be a subterfuge for discounting; rather they have to be a way of showing that we have skin in the game, that we are dedicated to delivering value, that we will share in the pain if we fall short, but that we will share in the rewards if we deliver outsized value."

The CMO and Consultant Perspective

Sometimes it is useful to take a step back from the relationship-building exercises of the day and ask those who serve as coaches to the profession, both those within and outside the firm, what they think makes a difference in developing these critical relationships between lawyers and their clients.

Natalie Loeb is the founder of Loeb Leadership Development Group and a highly regarded leadership coach who works with lawyers and C-suite executives. Like Charles Martin at Macfarlanes, she believes that emotional intelligence and connection are essential parts of the equation.

According to Natalie, the best way for partners to engage with clients is to be curious about their clients as individuals. She tells lawyers to make sure that they show their clients that they care about them as people, and that by doing so, it will make an important difference in building trust. "Try to get to know them one-on-one. Show a genuine interest and concern for your client's well being and success to establish a foundation of enduring trust and loyalty."

Norm Rubenstein, a marketing consultant who has been both a CMO and an advisor to many of the Am Law 200, believes that despite all of the lawyer rankings available to companies, the choice of which firm to hire for a given type of work or matter typically comes down to two things: service and chemistry. "It's not that expertise and experience are not vital, but now we know it accounts for only about half the decision. The other relationship elements have risen up to be even more important. I hear from clients all of the time, 'I do care about when you will get the assignment done, and the cost and the technology you will be using, but to me, all of that is a backdrop to the fundamental question.' And that fundamental question is whether you are continually demonstrating your appreciation of the firm's brand and your relationship with the lawyers who have entrusted you with their important matters. As we all learn, the law practice itself is a relationship-based enterprise based as much on trust as on skill," Norm says.

Norm built his own very successful marketing practice by focusing on relationships, rather than direct solicitations. "I never wanted for someone's phone to light up with my name and for them to have an automatic response of 'Oh no, what does he want?' I was more interested in calling to say 'I'll be in New York, let's have dinner or go to the theater.'"

"If you have other interests in common, there is a strong likelihood that over time your working relationships will evolve into friendships. Friendships have many different levels and layers. I have lots of professional friends with whom I feel close. They are people with whom I enjoy spending time and who have become a part of my circle. But whether our relationships have evolved to the point where I might say, 'Hey, let's go to Rome next week' or not, I still want to have a meaningful and mutually satisfying working relationship with all of my clients — one that goes beyond just sitting down and talking about an engagement, getting up, leaving the client's office, and then sending them an invoice," he says.

For lawyers, Norm says that if you are doing all of the right things, you are ingratiating yourself in a way that makes your clients confident to rely on you, and that reliance ideally translates into some degree of enduring connection. "I tell my clients that a lawyer's goal should be to become indispensable or invaluable to his or her clients in the course of helping them achieve the objectives that motivated them to seek out his or her unique skills and judgment in the first place."

While building and strengthening client relationships is generally an individually focused activity, there are firms that have developed sophisticated firm-wide Client Relationship Management programs. Often referred to as CRM programs — not to be confused with CRM technology applications — these programs help to facilitate a systematic and institutionalized focus on key clients. Lee Garfinkle at Allen & Overy, says, "One of our key market differentiators is our institutionalized approach to client service and addressing client needs. Our lawyers excel at providing exceptional client service, focusing on global needs, not just specific practices or products that they individually provide. Our client relationship managers are as client focused as an account manager would be in a consulting firm or corporation — which is a rarity in a law firm environment. They each are dedicated to only a small handful of clients and are responsible for understanding the client's global business, identifying needs, and measuring client satisfaction through development of their own relationships with the client. A program like this is a very powerful differentiator and requires a firm with strong leadership, a collaborative culture, and a long-term view of client relationships."

"Years ago, the firm's leaders had a vision that elements of legal services delivery and the legal ecosystem were changing and quickly 'unbundling,'" says Lee. "Through strong leadership with great vision, we developed services within the firm that would satisfy future client needs and ensure that we would be able to continue to serve our clients holistically. We also recognized that the risk of not adapting was that our long-term client relationships could be potentially impacted. We now have groups in the firm that deliver legal advice through advanced technological and resourcing solutions. One example is Peerpoint, which is our global legal outsourcing platform. We also have our Legal Services Center in Belfast, which provides our clients with cost-effective resourcing for large matters. We've also recognized the growing importance of technology in the delivery of legal services so we have opened our own technology space called Fuse. Fuse isn't a place for us to house and incubate future clients, it's a space where we along with our clients and innovative technology companies can collaborate to explore, develop and test legal, regulatory and deal-related technology solutions."

Despina Kartson, currently Global Director, Business Development and Communications at Jones Day, has been a CMO at some of the world's leading law firms. She believes that key to a law firm's ability to retain its best clients are client service, legal skills and knowledge. "Client service is essential, and that means being incredibly responsive, and delivering on client expectations. Relationship lawyers must be adept at properly handling and staffing matters, being expert at proactive communications, and problem-solving. These skills have significant value and contribute to how a client feels working with the lawyer. Of course, lawyers must have both the ability and the interest in working to go deep and understand the client's business and their sector."

Jeff Berardi is the CMO of K&L Gates LLP, and one of the pioneers in the use of including sales professionals in the marketing mix. Jeff has created a client-facing team of professionals working closely in concert with partners and potential clients to generate leads for new business. "As a CMO, I see clearly that getting to know clients makes a huge difference in recommending how we as a firm interface with our marketing. Clients, above all, want to know that their law firm is paying close attention and valuing the relationship," he says.

Carol Schiro Greenwald, a coach and consultant to many individual law firm partners, says, "Today's clients want to be involved in the decision-making related to their matter. They want their lawyers to know their world and understand their individual position, and they expect them to partner with them. It's crucial that the lawyer knows what impact the work they are doing will have on the client and how it may impact the client's life, job and future."

Carol explains that when she meets with her coaching clients, there are three essential areas she covers. "First, lawyers need to understand twenty-first century clients. They need to change their own attitude. They need to see the value in clients, not just to the bottom line, but also in terms of the knowledge the client can add to a matter since they know more about their situation and its history than any outside lawyer."

"Second, lawyers need to revamp their writing, avoiding legalese and instead use business English whenever they can. When clients get to unfamiliar legal phrases or abbreviations, they stop reading.

Retainer agreements, memos, invoices, and emails all need to be in understandable English."

"Last," she says, "they need to befriend their client between engagements to see what's new, visiting the client's company, joining their industry or professional associations, introducing them to people they think will be useful for the client to know, recommending the client for an industry or community honor, supporting their charities, and offering them visibility in their content offerings, such as a quote in an article or a guest piece."

Yolanda Cartusciello of PP&C Consulting has done a lot of work with law firms, taking them through a process called client journey mapping. Client journey mapping is not innovative for the business world, but it is for law firms. She helps take firms through the steps that a client might take in selecting a law firm for a given matter. Ultimately, there should be a massive "aha" moment when the lawyer starts to think like a client, looking at problems from the client's point of view. "That is vital in all of the discussions we have about building relationships," says Yolanda. "You have to think in terms of the client's perspective. What our process does is help demonstrate to the lawyer how the client thinks about this piece. They need to see this and figure out the solutions for themselves."

Aric Press, Yolanda's partner at PP&C Consulting and the former editor of the *American Lawyer* says, "I'm more convinced than ever that this remains a relationship business, so to the degree you can reinforce those relationships, you are doing your job as a marketer. Marketing efforts don't have to be innovative; they just need to successfully get service providers together with those who need the service."

Yolanda says, "Client teams are popular, but we have heard stories about success and failure. Firm management needs to have a view as to what they want to get out of the team concept. Maybe it is to expand the relationship 5% or it may be about creating succession plans." Yolanda points out, "The best client teams start with a client interview. What does the client think of the existing work and current team?"

Bill Carter of ALM spends a lot of time thinking about the relationships that drive clients to law firms. He points out that the data and metrics that are now available are incredible and while they may not be the driver of a relationship, they certainly may be a consideration in the firm selection process. "The world is very much online so while lawyers need to have that relationship with key clients, they should know that their clients can now use data and metrics, including rankings, survey results and other reviews, to see where a law firm or lawyer fits in the marketplace." Bill states that ALM is working on putting data in one place to look at firm comparisons of work product, activity work recognition, awards, win/loss and an array of fifteen data points. He believes that the availability of data will likely play an increasingly important role in the client-law firm equation and factor into the process of selecting and retaining a lawyer.

Think Piece

Today, As Always, Relationships Are What Matter

By Norm Rubenstein*

While the business of law firms has always been about developing and managing relationships, the stakes for creating enduring relationships have never been as high as they are today.

I attribute this to three causes: (1) an increasingly competitive global marketplace that offers people with the authority to hire outside counsel myriad options; (2) a savvier universe of in-house decision makers, most of whom have first-hand experience working in law firms; and (3) a continually intensifying sea change in the legal marketplace that, since 2008, continually has redefined "excellent" law firm performance.

Technology is partly responsible for the more level playing field on which law firms compete for clients, providing general counsel, business owners, and others who hire lawyers and law firms easier access to a wider array of service providers, domestically and internationally. And, at the same time that technological progress has made it easier for clients to choose and work with firms in other geographies, law firms also have been expanding their footprints, hoping to persuade clients, both extant and new, that their physical presence in other locations makes them more desirable.

---

* Norm Rubenstein, a partner in the consulting firm Zeughauser Group, is widely regarded as one of the legal industry's most experienced and innovative strategists. A former chief marketing officer for three global law firms and an inaugural inductee into the Legal Marketing Association's Hall of Fame, he collaborates with law firm leaders to increase client and market share, create and launch effective branding initiatives, and assess and enhance marketing organizations and investments.

But perhaps the most important reason why law firms of all sizes and in every segment of the marketplace are refocusing their attention on relationship development and enhancement is that the decision makers they are serving or pitching have expanded their expectations of outside counsel, in turn making it increasingly difficult to convert current client satisfaction into long-term loyalty. Recent Acritas data,[1] for example, suggest that as important as experience and expertise remain among the selection criteria for choosing outside counsel, today's clients are equally focused on a law firm's approach to matter management and to service delivery and on its demonstrable business-savviness.

The parallel rise of LPOs and other competitors for the work law firms once took for granted is further evidence of the tectonic-plate shifting that has defined the legal marketplace for close to a decade. Clients want substance and quality as much as they always did, but now they care as much about efficiency, predictability, and value as they do about perceived expertise. The quest for those attributes has expanded the universe of providers they consider for certain kinds of services, in the process changing the way that certain kinds of work is delivered and, with those changes, the legal marketplace itself. Firms whose names have always been synonymous with market leadership are learning that change in the legal marketplace is inexorable, and embracing change is as much a strategy for survival as for success.

Over the years, I have asked successful lawyers with whom I have worked the same question: what was your path to success and were you guided by good advice from your mentors? And, unfailingly, virtually all were taught that if they approached client relationships thoughtfully and unstintingly, those relationships ideally would deepen and strengthen, transmuting from something purely transactional to an enduring bond capable of withstanding

---

1.   Sharplegal U.S. 2017, reported Jan. 2018 by Acritas Research Ltd.

the marketing incursions of competitors. In other words, they were advised to become their clients' "trusted advisors."

Sadly, there is no single formula for that process: clients, like law firms, have different preferences and priorities in the same way that law firms have different cultures and personalities. They expect outside counsel to accommodate those preferences and priorities, whether in a bill format, an alternative-pricing mechanism, an idiosyncratic definition of responsiveness, or some value-additive contribution, such as a secondment or a customized CLE.

"Trusted advisors" share some attributes that are inherent, not learned, and for which there are no substitutes: excellent judgment and sincerity top that list. But I am convinced that lawyers who possess those attributes and who also are as gifted at relationship development and customized service delivery as they are at delivering excellent legal and business results have the ultimate marketplace advantage. By "investing" wholeheartedly in their clients' successes and priorities, they earn their clients' loyalty, and with it, the truly enduring relationships that should be every law firm partner's primary objective.

Chapter 4

Culture and Pursuing New Business

There are law firms at which collaboration is part of the firm's DNA. Partners meet with one another over lunch to explore finding opportunities to work together and better serve clients. They introduce one another to prospects for all types of networking and new business scenarios. Then there are firms down the block where lawyers are involved in a whole different world. It's a dog-eat-dog, kill-or-be-killed environment, like footage from an episode of *Game of Thrones*. Guess which approach is more likely to lead to developing business?

Heidi K. Gardner, PhD, the author of "Smart Collaboration,"[1] is a former McKinsey consultant, Harvard Business School professor and current Distinguished Fellow at Harvard Law School. Her research demonstrates that when specialists collaborate across functional boundaries, great things happen. Firms earn higher margins, inspire greater client loyalty, attract and retain the best talent, and gain a competitive edge. Heidi says, "Empirical research demonstrates that partners who engage in smart collaboration — that is, join up their specialized expertise with partners' complementary

---

1.   Harvard Business Review Press (2017).

53

knowledge to address clients' complex problems — are more than four times more productive in business development than their less collaborative peers. The better collaborators achieve not only higher revenues and profits in the near term, but also generate stickier relationships with clients that even sustain external shocks like a downturn. So their return on investment on business development efforts pays out higher, longer."

"The better collaborators achieve not only higher revenues and profits in the near term, but also generate stickier relationships with clients that even sustain external shocks like a downturn. So their return on investment on business development efforts pays out higher, longer."

—Heidi K. Gardner, PhD, Harvard Law School

What are the keys to producing a law firm culture of collaboration and one that encourages business development? Is it a firm's leadership, or is it a set of articulated hiring standards used to recruit lawyers and staff? Is it the overall brand and ethos of the firm, or is it the compensation structure?

Culture within a law firm is comprised of all of these things. It's the small everyday actions that take place inside of a firm that demonstrate the organization's leadership values and the behaviors it wants to reinforce. If a firm states on its website and in its recruiting materials that it fosters a collegial and family-friendly environment, but in reality, its associates and staff rarely get home to see their spouses, what is the true culture of the firm? In many ways, particularly when it comes to building and reinforcing law firm culture, actions speak much louder than words.

Culture: What Does It Mean?

If culture is a critical driver of behavior and revenue, it is important to look at the part it plays in creating an environment that encourages marketing. A firm leader may say that he or she promotes collaboration between partners in order to provide the best service to existing clients. The leader may even encourage partners to cross-sell services. But if the firm's compensation system does not reward working together, and partners are rewarded solely on business origination or on a murky compensation metric, the collaboration message a firm leader espouses at the annual partner retreat will fall on deaf ears. In fact, sending mixed messages about what the firm values — e.g., a sentiment of "we care about each other and treat one another with respect" paired with a singular "what you originate is what you keep" ethos — will likely cause confusion and resentment.

Some fundamental questions that law firm leaders and marketers should ask themselves when thinking about firm culture, are:

- What do you want the firm to stand for?
- How do you differentiate yourself and the firm from others with which it competes?
- How do you communicate and reinforce your beliefs?
- Do your benefits and compensation for staff, associates and partners align with your cultural values?
- Are your partners, associates and staff able to articulate your firm's mission and how the firm differentiates itself?
- Is the desired behavior — that which is valued and communicated as being expected — rewarded?

- Are your partners, particularly those in leadership and supervisory positions, acting in ways that are consistent with the culture you want to drive?

- Do you treat your administrative staff with equal regard as you do your legal professionals?

Proskauer partner Ralph Ferrara says "Today, regardless of what you call it, it's generally an eat-what-you-kill law firm world. There is always a scramble. 'Who is the billing and responsible partner?' That puts a big damper on business development. No one wants to lose the relationship. Firms should compensate partners based on how supportive they are of the work of others. Leaders, like those at Proskauer, reinforce the message by demonstrating that the way to advance in the firm is with the support and help of other partners."

Leadership consultant Natalie Loeb of Loeb Leadership Development Group often leverages a toolbox of assessments — including the Myers-Briggs personality assessment and the DiSC® work style assessment — when she helps to identify how differing personalities work within firm cultures. She then maps out a plan to help individual partners and senior managers realize their leadership potential and model their desired behaviors. Natalie has seen effective leadership strengthen firm culture and believes that building a marketing culture that is intentional beyond the compensation system can make a difference. She shows that intentionally planning to have a particular (i.e., supportive, risk-taking, innovative) culture will impact how confident people are in developing business and creating their own practice. Natalie points out what happens when firms don't pursue cultural objectives. She says, "If you don't intentionally think about and create a culture, a culture will create itself. And it may not be the one you want."

The imperative to define and focus on culture is even more so the case today with firms experiencing sudden changes due to shifts in the legal profession. Between transient leadership and a carousel of lateral hires, maintaining a consistent and solid culture is a tough task.

Consider what occurs when there is a change in leadership. One law firm leader may believe in collaboration and communication throughout the ranks of the firm. This leader walks the halls, knows everyone's name, and often hosts groups of associates in her office to brainstorm solutions for the firm's clients. In working with associates, she talks about the importance of building relationships with their professional community and staying in touch with alumni. She works closely with her CMO and involves him or her in firm strategy. But what if a new leader takes over, someone with a substantial practice load and less of a comfort level with managing people? The new leader may be more of an introvert who prefers less social interaction. She may prefer not to hold meetings with associates and may have never met many of the firm's clients outside of the circle of his own practice. She may not like working directly with any members of the C-suite but instead relegates all discussions on operational issues through a Chief Operating Officer or Executive Director. What will this change in leadership style do to a firm's culture?

Through their actions, leaders send messages to the organizations they lead, letting employees know what its leadership values and what it will reward. Cultures develop based on those messages.

A similar scenario, no less impactful, comes when there are changes lower down on the organizational ladder. Having laterals or senior staff people join a firm can also be a jolt to the culture.

Identifying the behaviors and personality types you want to hire and attract, in advance of the recruiting process, makes a big difference in the culture a firm produces. Onboarding processes, including introducing the recruits into projects and acquainting them with fellow employees early on in the process, can also help the new hire succeed within the firm culture.

"Firm leaders build a culture by identifying the model they want and then constantly reinforcing and reminding people of it," says Natalie.

Firm culture and brand are interrelated: It is a firm's culture that ultimately becomes a core element in the brand. Consultant Norm

Rubenstein of Zeughauser Group says, "This doesn't just have to come from the top of the organization but rather it has to come from and be displayed throughout an organization."

Branding is an experience that has to be uniform across everything from the performance of the mailroom clerk to the firm's partnership. If the firm has a snarky receptionist or a diffident accounting person, it sets a tone. Bad behavior that is tolerated is in essence rewarded, and that creates a culture. Culture is not just an intellectual concept. It's an experiential one.

In addition to structuring a firm compensation system with drivers that reward collaboration, there are other things that a leader can do to produce a culture that supports marketing:

Lead by example: If firm leaders champion and work with the marketing department, others will follow suit.

Speak about it: At each partner meeting and retreat, the leader should devote a few minutes (at least) to talk about some aspect of the firm's marketing and business development efforts. It should be a line item on every agenda.

Applaud good behavior: If leaders see successes in business development and collaboration, kudos should be given to those who participate. Leaders can use those wins to launch conversations within the lawyer ranks about why collaboration and business development are critical to the firm's success.

Show up: Face time is essential. Leaders need to show their support by being present at firm-wide business development events.

Meet with clients: Leaders should let their partners know that they welcome the chance to meet with the firm's clients. Even if the firm does not conduct formal client surveys, there are other ways to demonstrate to clients that the firm's leadership cares.

A great example of a firm leader who cares about culture is Henry Nassau, the Chief Executive Officer of Dechert LLP. While many successful people start their day with a morning routine involving exercise or catching up on the overnight news, Henry has six questions that he asks of himself each morning.

"When I first wake up, I always think of these questions," says Henry. "The first is 'What am I supposed to be doing?' because my primary job is to make everyone in the firm, and I mean *everyone*, more successful. The second thing I think about is 'How do I help to continue to grow the revenue of the firm?' because if you're not growing revenue, you're not providing the opportunity for great service for clients and career paths for talent. Third, I think about 'How do I deal with underperforming partners who may need more help at the firm?' Fourth, 'How do we make the associate experience even more rewarding?' In an age when the average associate stays at a firm for about two-and-a-half years, I want associates to think, 'This is a great place and where I really want to be.' And fifth, 'How do we create an even more inclusive culture?' An inclusive environment is very important to me, as I feel certain that a diverse workplace is a better one for all of us and gives us the best thinking from an array of people. And then the last — and at times the most important — question is, 'Are we making sure everyone has fun and enjoys being part of the firm?'"

Part of Henry's cultural drive is to create a collegial culture that embraces an exchange of ideas. "I hold client team meetings for all of my key clients, where everybody at the firm who touches the particular client, from first-year associates on up to partners, is expected to attend." Henry's meetings are a way for a whole team to better understand the client and its business.

"It's an early morning breakfast meeting, so you have to make sure it's engaging enough that people want to be there," says Henry. "We go around and talk about everything we're doing for the client so that everybody has a good overview of what is taking place. And somebody may have an idea for the client and say, 'Yes, but have you thought about this?' And so it forces the group to talk and work together as a team. There is a big benefit to being inclusive and learning from many different perspectives. My one and only sacrosanct rule is that everybody in the room has to contribute to the conversation. We also make sure that the meeting does not run longer than an hour."

In sum, these meetings facilitate the sharing of knowledge, allow lawyers to feel involved, and help avoid having that awkward instance when a partner has to say to a client, "I'm sorry, I don't know anything about that. But why don't I call Jane to find out more?"

As for sending a message to the rest of the firm, Henry encourages his partners to have similar meetings focusing on their own clients. "It helps the client," says Henry. "And it certainly helps those at the firm."

Allen Parker, the former leader of Cravath, Swaine & Moore, and now the General Counsel of Wells Fargo in San Francisco, strongly believes in the need to care about all the individuals who work for an organization. At Cravath, Allen walked the walk and went out of his way to keep the firm a friendly and supportive place both for staff and for associates. One of his traditions was a series of breakfast meetings he would hold for the entire class of new associates, typically with about eight associates at each meeting. In true Allen style, he was always prepared for these get-togethers. Prior to a meeting, he would read all the associates' biographies and then, at the breakfasts, ask them questions about their academic background and interests. He tried to know enough about all the associates to connect with them personally and to enable them to connect with each other.

The associates loved spending time with Allen. I would sometimes run into associates as they returned from an Allen Parker breakfast, and they would say, "Wow, he really spent the time to get to know us. He knows my name and about my work back in law school." And they were so excited and motivated. It meant so much to them. These breakfasts became an important and authentic contribution to maintaining the firm's culture.

The Marketer's Role

Lara Day is the Chief Culture and Communications Officer at Brownstein Hyatt Farber Schreck, LLP, headquartered in Denver. While she joined the firm initially as its Director of Communications, she is now responsible for researching, cultivating and preserving Brownstein's organizational culture.

Lara explains that there were two factors that led to Brownstein's cultural initiative. First, with the firm's fiftieth anniversary approaching, the firm leadership continued to think about the firm's future. They wondered, like other firms, what the next generation of partners would be like once the firm's founders were gone, and how they could ensure they were maintaining the strong culture that allowed the firm to thrive for the first fifty years.

Second, the leadership was inspired by Simon Sinek's "Leaders Eat Last," a book about the role of leadership and the impact of culture. The book was recommended by one of Lara's friends who answered her annual query about favorite books of the past year. After Lara and others at the firm read it and understood more about the importance of culture, they decided to start their cultural initiative. "We were inspired to do something, and we understood it was about more than cupcakes and foosball tables," says Lara.

Lara knows that without the support of leadership and their express buy-in, the program, now in its fifth year, would not have moved forward. The first year they conducted a firm values survey. "We really needed to understand and get the secret sauce down on paper. Part of that meant unveiling what values people had at the firm and what they cared about. Making use of those values and speaking about them in an educational sense is essential. They needed to believe in those values and understand that we must recruit, promote, evaluate, share feedback, and make everyday business decisions based on those values," says Lara. Now, at most meetings that Lara attends, partners integrate talk of those values into their conversations.

Jennifer Scalzi, President of Calibrate Legal, Inc., believes that the CMO can also play an important role in solidifying and communicating values. "The CMO should act as the instigator of forward movement for their firm. In the future, we'll continue to see greater emphasis on the client experience, which by and large falls into the domain of marketing. Under the umbrella of 'client experience,' the responsibility to maintain the culture falls on virtually all internal services, from HR to the Library to Finance and Facilities," says Jennifer.

Jennifer believes that clients and employees first experience the firm's brand from the top down, but that the CMO should ensure the experience is consistent by serving as a chief curator of culture and ideas. The CMO should be the one helping to lead forward-thinking conversations across the organization based on his or her understanding of client-purchasing behavior and market trends.

The CMO can be very influential in explaining to the partners how to use communications tactics to support the culture. As many in this role have a communications background, they understand the power of the word and the tone of accessibility.

A Culture of Training

Macfarlanes is a firm known for producing high-quality legal work. That reputation results from recruiting the very best entry-level "trainees," and perhaps, more importantly, from the intensive training they provide to all new attorneys.

As is the case with most British firms, the trainee is brought in as an apprentice. Charles Martin, Senior Partner at Macfarlanes says, "All of the trainees are actively mentored by senior lawyers and partners and all of them share offices with a senior lawyer or a partner. The focus is very much on learning on the job. They are not just being tasked to perform menial grunt work. They are here to learn by watching and participating."

Macfarlanes is well-served in the UK by the training system. Unlike the United States where first-year associates are highly paid and have high expectations for the work they will be handling, the system for the most part in the UK is a different one. "The trainee is paid less than a newly qualified lawyer and part of that is because there is a contract, a deal between the trainee and the firm, that they are there partly for their own benefit and to receive training," says Charles.

Training isn't just an adjunct to the practice of law at Macfarlanes. It is intrinsically woven into what the firm is, and that starts even before training with how it recruits. Charles says, "We are essentially applying, at the earliest stage, the test of 'Do we think that this person has potential to be a partner in the firm?' We are not just looking for valued foot soldiers. We want the people we recruit to have what it takes to become the stars and owners of the firm in the long run."

While we have heard that the millennial and younger generations may be less focused on achieving partnership or even pursuing legal careers, Macfarlanes focuses on finding a disproportionate number of young trainees who see the world somewhat differently. "They are very motivated and do get the fact that by coming here they will get training that is more likely to equip them to be trusted advisors and well-rounded lawyers," says Charles.

"There is a focus on legal concepts that maybe some other places do not have to quite the same extent. Alongside that training, we do get them up to speed on soft skills development and other aspects of being a successful lawyer," he says.

Reinforcing Firm Culture

In large established law firms, cultural changes may take years to take place, but what happens with younger firms? Can an intentional culture be built from the ground up?

Andrew Stamelman is a partner and one of the founders of the law firm Sherman, Wells, Sylvester & Stamelman LLP. The firm was founded just four years ago, in New York and New Jersey, but most of its partners had worked together for many years at another larger New Jersey law firm. "Because we are on the young side in terms of growing an organization, retention of top talent is very important to us and so is providing the very best in client service," says Andrew. "Fortunately, we find that those two priorities work well together."

How have the firm's leaders built their culture? Andrew and others in leadership roles make sure that they each involve associates in the process of client care. "We need to ensure that we are really growing the strength of all of the lawyers who work for us, not just the partners. Our success as a law firm will not be measured based on the reputation of our senior-most partners ten years from now, but whether we are successful in promoting the role and reputation of younger attorneys who will provide legs to our firm well beyond the retirement of our now senior leaders. Recognizing this, we have from the outset, focused on mentoring and promoting our younger lawyers, and it is paying off."

"It is so important to avoid egos in this business," says Andrew. "There's a temptation to treasure client and referral relationships so much that you keep them to yourself. That may seem natural, but everyone seems to win something when you share the exposure with a younger partner or associate. Clients appreciate seeing the quality of the lawyers on their team and have comfort in knowing you have a deep bench. The same thing is true with referral sources: the more that can be done to expand and deepen relationships with referral sources, the more significant these relationships become for the firm. I suppose that there is a risk in opening up clients and referral sources to younger lawyers, but the benefits are worth these limited risks."

At Sherman Wells, even their offices speak to the culture. There are no corner offices in the firm and everyone from the senior partner to the newest associate has the same furniture. When the space was being constructed, the founding partners wanted lawyers and staff to feel inspired to think creatively and do great work, so they created an atmosphere that helps them do just that. To that end, the office walls are filled with the work of Bob Gruen, a client and famed rock and roll photographer known for his iconographic shots of John Lennon, Debbie Harry, and other rock legends.

Intentional culture is something that comes from the top. Starting a new firm gives inaugural leaders an excellent opportunity to set the tone. Andrew advises young lawyers about the importance of being visible and building a personal brand so that when someone meets a lawyer for the first time, that person already knows he or she has a good reputation. This broad exposure may come from public speaking, writing articles, or being active in the bar association or non-profit community. He also sees the importance of fostering close third-party relationships. According to Andrew, this is where client referrals come from. As someone who represents a number of very successful family-run and middle-market companies, he often interacts with other types of professionals, such as financial advisors, insurance professionals or accountants. "I've become friends with many of these professionals who I have worked closely with over the years, as I tend to nurture relationships with those who are not only good people, but also do great work for my clients. If you had a good experience with someone whom you genuinely like, and it's a great fit for your client, you'll make the introduction. When these same referral sources feel similarly about me and about our firm, they send their clients our way."

"I also make sure to introduce associates to clients and other advisors. It's important to bring them in and make those supportive connections with our clients intrinsic in the relationship," says Andrew, for whom much of his business comes from clients he's represented for over thirty years. "The things you enjoy the most are the things that genuinely make the relationship deeper. Clients who think the world of you will tell their friends and that's a great way of getting business. I want our firm's associates to be a part of that."

Jeff Klein, who heads the Employment Litigation practice group at Weil Gotshal, offers advice on how individual partners can work to maintain a firm culture that rewards business development while still encouraging collaboration. "Personally, I follow two core tenets in my day-to-day business development efforts. First, have a long memory, but reward support and collaboration in the short term. Second, find ways to pay opportunities forward to colleagues, but hold them accountable for making the most of the opportunity," he says.

What does this mean in practice? Jeff explained, "On the first tenet, it means keeping track of opportunities you helped develop for colleagues, even those that didn't lead anywhere, while celebrating success stories by, for example, enabling the affected colleague to work in a substantial role on the new engagement, introducing him or her to decision-makers at the client, and memorializing for law firm leadership the details of his or her contributions and value."

"Eventually, you may be able to arrange for your colleague to open the next matter and give him or her a sense of ownership in the client relationship," Jeff says. "The second tenet is focused on communicating directly with your colleagues. Even at the risk of annoying them, bring them opportunities — whether for potential new work, introductions, referrals, or even a favor for a client — and explain how it could benefit them to get involved. Then, follow up with them on these opportunities while making clear that you would love to contribute to the growth of their practices through cross-selling or helping clients in need."

K&L Gates has done a lot to try to instill a culture in support of business development and sales. The firm was an early adopter of client team programs, just over a decade ago. Today, it has a number of marketing department team members who work in client development/sales roles; these professionals are typically not lawyers but instead have expertise in business development and sales. These client development professionals help identify potential clients and conduct client feedback interviews, often spending a large percentage of their time making introductions between potential clients and the firm.

The sales team is just one element in an overall program to encourage client development. K&L Gates CMO Jeff Berardi continually presents client development workshops to the firm. Partners are also asked to do an annual individual development plan to track their business development pursuits, and for new partners, the plan is mandatory. The sales team and planning process are championed by firm leadership and woven into the fabric of the firm's culture.

Tim Corcoran, a consultant who advises firms on project management and process improvement, says, "Culture is critical in so many ways. But how do you rebuild that culture? It's long-standing, and you can't just change it overnight. If you have a set of owners who are opposed to operating in a certain way, I would dial back my expectations. They may never change. But if they want to change, and their incentives are aligned, they may well start collaborating."

Building a Culture to Support Business Development

By Silvia L. Coulter*

Culture is not simply a trend; it's a way of living day to day at a law firm. It embodies principles of conduct and behavior that apply to everyone. There are sophisticated assessments in fact which measure the culture at a firm and pinpoint areas where there are weak links. To ensure the firm's culture facilitates new client acquisition, client retention, and client growth, here are some best practices which have stood the test of time from inside and outside of the legal industry.

Align compensation with expectations.

This is a difficult one for many firms. We tend to reward individual behavior: X billable hour expectations, X dollar book of business to become and remain an equity partner, participation on firm committees, and other requirements. Yet, to build a strong and long-lasting sales culture and one that both grows and retains clients, it is critical to reward team participation. Whether it's another point or another dollar, rewarding partners for the behavior the firm is seeking to achieve is critical. Not expanding the relationships will hurt the key relationship partner in the long run, even if the relationship partner doesn't see it that way. In one Am Law 50 firm that I've studied, the message is loud and clear — collaborate:

---

*   Silvia L. Coulter is a Principal of LawVision Group LLC. Silvia is an expert in helping law firms grow their revenue and assists with client acquisition, client retention, and client growth. She works with firms on their business development, leadership, and collaboration goals.

team, team, team. Yet the compensation system is still not aligned with the message and therefore the expectations fall short and the partners are not living up to their or the firm's potential. Align compensation with expectations, and results will follow.

Share the client; grow the client.

Sharing clients — or as some firms call it, "cross-selling" — is a significant challenge. Most partners will say they are not good at this for the simple reason that they do not have the right contact at the client organization. Our response to that? Well, then ask the client or your contact at the client, "Who handles IP, or Corporate, or other areas?"

The next issue is one of trust. Do I trust my IP partner in the Chicago office not to mess this up? To facilitate client growth, it is imperative to create a culture of trust among the partners. One way to do this (there are many, of course) is to hold regular luncheons by video or in person across practices to discuss specific clients and to introduce partners on a continual basis to one another. The Marketing and Business Development Department at any firm is one of the best resources for these activities. They see the firm from a bird's-eye view and have a strong understanding on what is going on in which offices and for which clients.

Still, some partners will not expand the relationships, even if they are approached by another partner whom they know and trust. Protecting one's turf is never a good idea. Sometimes it's too late when partners realize this and they've lost the client altogether. The more one shares clients, the better off one's chances are to retain the clients. This is a proven statistic across firms. Further, those partners who do have relationships with a large client will pursue those relationships regardless of the partner who "owns" the client. So, working toward client growth with others in the firm who have relationships across the client organization is the best way to build a team, ensure a collaborative culture, and to retain the client. This needs to be a top-down focus in the firm and a requirement of partners.

Service excellence takes a village.

To truly create a culture of service excellence, which in turn leads to client retention, client growth, and often more profitable work, everyone must work together and see the firm and the legal work through the eyes of their clients. Does everything speak XXX dollars per hour at the firm? A client service team includes everyone who "touches" the client, including assistants, paralegals, associates, partners, and others who provide resources to the client. Be inclusive of all team members — professionals and staff, and the service levels will increase significantly.

Strong leadership builds collaborative cultures.

A collaborative culture depends on strong and good leadership. Modeling team behavior leads to improved teamwork all around. There are many leaders in law firms: the Executive Committee, the Managing Partner, office Managing Partners, Practice and Department Chairs, operations team leaders, and client team leaders, to name most. These leaders are all responsible for acting in a collaborative and supportive manner and for facilitating a culture of collaboration.

For client teams, there are still some areas for improvement, namely, adding a business development manager role to the team and meeting regularly with the members of the team to discuss ways in which they are or can collaborate among themselves and with the client. Reviewing partner business development plans and seeing where they are year-to-date with those plans makes a difference in encouraging partners to work harder to achieve their business development goals. Try to demonstrate through leadership that everyone's efforts matter. It's also wise to remove non-collaborative partners quickly from positions of authority. Modeling good behavior is an essential element for building strong and collaborative cultures.

Recognition is important.

There is more than one form of recognition (which is often just compensation). Since firms are not likely to recognize partners or other firm members who do things to support a collaborative culture, it often does not happen. We as humans respond to reward. It is wise to recognize good habits, small successes, teamwork, and going the extra mile. Every time. Expecting and recognizing good behaviors drives other good behaviors. Corporations (law firms' clients) are very good at this. For example, an extra partnership point matters. Recognizing teamwork through shared credit matters. Call outs at partner meetings recognizing teamwork or extra efforts matters. Try to incorporate recognition into the firm's culture and the difference in performance will be noticeable.

Training supports firm goals.

Whether it is leadership, team work, or business development, a collaborative culture depends on having the proper training in these areas to drive expected results. Many firms have sent their leaders to executive leadership programs at various universities or hired leadership development coaches to help teach important team and leader skills. Business development training and coaching is another area in which firms are investing training dollars. A good trainer/coach will push individuals to cooperate with others as a team to drive results.

In summary, to build a collaborative culture requires taking a 360-degree look at the firm and assessing areas for growth. Collaborative cultures will attract and retain more clients, more talent to service those clients, and create a happier and healthier work environment for all.

Chapter 5

Building a Marketing Department and Hiring the Right CMO

Evolution of the CMO Role

Recently, I had breakfast with a group of CMOs from several national law firms. We reminisced how when many of us started in this business two decades ago, none of the lawyers understood how marketing could help their firms. It was a brand-new profession.

In those early years, we were often frustrated. We didn't feel we had any say on firm strategy nor did we have access to essential data, such as firm financials. But the firms and their lawyers were not to blame. Legal marketing was a new area. In the beginning, as with any startup, the marketing heads were wearing many hats, creating new business pitches, answering press calls, and assisting with internal communications. Looking back, while it was a struggle, it was great training and exposure to the many areas and core tactics that comprise law firm marketing.

The profession has matured over the years, but while there have been huge advances in how the role of the CMO operates, for some, the same struggles for marketers remain inside of law firms. The Legal Marketing Association (LMA) is now thirty years old and continues to be the authority on all matters relating to legal marketing. Hundreds of people in the legal marketing profession, including all levels of marketing staff, consultants and vendors, attend the LMA annual conference. While today the conversation has advanced to topics such as the use of AI, process improvement, and the impact of legal operations within the in-house counsel's department, many of the hallway conversations still echo themes of the past. Marketers still report that many of the lawyers with whom they work still lack clarity on how marketing can advance their practices, or why it is that the marketing department needs access to financial information and resources to operate their programs.

Today, there are still law firm leaders who hire CMOs stating they want the individual to simply build a proper infrastructure or "fix the plumbing." At those firms, the role of CMO and their staff is still considered heavily tactical and administrative.

There are still those leaders who believe the CMO should spend 100% of his or her efforts making sure new business pitches include the most up-to-date deals and cases, that Chambers, Legal 500, and Lawdragon rankings are reflective of the firm's work, and that press calls are answered.

While all of these things need to be managed, it's akin to saying to a litigator, "Please make sure that you have enough legal-sized paper in the copy machine." Yes, of course, basic tasks need to be handled before a firm becomes more strategic, but most marketers, especially CMOs, are capable of so much more. According to a recent study produced by Bloomberg Law and the Legal Marketing Association, more than a quarter of the responding CMOs wanted to play a larger part in the firm's strategic planning.[1]

Amanda K. Brady, Managing Partner and Global Practice Leader, Law Firm Management Practice, at the legal recruiting

---

1.   Where Are We Now? Revealing the Latest Trends in Legal Marketing and Business Development Results from a joint Legal Marketing Association and Bloomberg Law research study—April 2018, https://www.legalmarketing.org/page/2018-lma-bloomberg-law-research-study.

firm of Major, Lindsey & Africa, points out that at most success-ful firms, the CMO role has changed. "There's been an evolution. There is now an expectation that the individual is commercially minded and understands the business of the firm," she says.

Amanda and others see that the CMO needs to be involved at both the firm-wide and the practice level in order to affect change. She says, "The CMO should be a part of all discussions regarding the firm's business strategy, including talent acquisition. He or she may not be responsible for bringing in the individual, but if a prac-tice wants to grow, the CMO should be there helping firms formu-late a plan for growth and designing a strategy to integrate acqui-sitions, whether individuals or entire firms. The talent pool and the expertise you are looking for — everything comes back to firm strategy. That's where the CMO can genuinely add value."

Why Do CMOs Have a Tough Time?

Being a CMO at a law firm can be extremely rewarding but there certainly are challenges to the role as well, as previously noted. Various factors can impede a CMO's success at a given firm, for any of the following reasons.

1. *The CMO might not be a good fit for the firm.* Typically, the deci-sion makers in charge of hiring CMOs are not themselves mar-keting experts. When you have people interviewing applicants or overseeing a marketing position and they are unfamiliar with mar-keting practices and strategy, the marketing process may be skewed to favor incorrect factors.

2. *Marketers are often the first ones to spot problems that firm man-agement would rather not face.* Law firm partners may not want to hear, for example, messages regarding the need for succession planning for key client accounts or be told that they should be accountable for developing business. Marketers can become pretty unpopular when they are simply stating the truth about the firm's weaknesses.

3. *Marketers who are not involved in strategic decision-making may become frustrated.* Marketers are, much like lawyers, advocates for the firms that hire them. They take their jobs seriously and will go to the mat for the partners who employ them. Jennifer Scalzi of Calibrate Legal points out one of the reasons for marketing turnover. "Marketing professionals, on the whole, are a passionate bunch. For many, getting a seat at the table has been an uphill (and often ongoing) battle, and so the success or failure of the programs they shepherd can be both emotional and highly personal," she says.

4. *Firms may not provide adequate resources to marketing.* Based on marketing industry standards, a typical firm should spend between 3%–7% of annual revenue on marketing efforts, but according to a recent study by BTI, in 2017, the typical law firm will spend 2.53% of firm revenue on marketing and business development.[2] Bearing in mind that the items included within that budget, such as client entertainment expenses, may vary from firm to firm, the fact remains that there are firms with hundreds of lawyers that operate with small, overstretched marketing staffs.

Still, there are exciting challenges and great opportunities for the role of the CMO. Much depends on how the firm's management communicates and works with their CMO, and how involved the CMO is as a part of the management team.

Hiring the Right CMO

What should law firm management do to ensure they are hiring the right person for this critical role?

---

2.   BTI Guide to Maximum Marketing & Business Development 2017: The 10 Strategies Driving Pacesetting Performance at Law Firms, https://www.bticonsulting.com/marketing-and-business-development-strategies/.

1. *Skills and Chemistry:* Most important, firms need to hire candidates with the right skill set. If you were to look at a pool of 100 CMO candidates and conduct a skill assessment, you might find twenty key skill sets within the whole group. If you look closer, you find that each person has just ten of those skills, and out of those, they have those skills in varying ratios. No one CMO candidate has the same exact skills as the next, and if they do have common skills, those ratios will vary widely. Does a firm need someone who is skilled at editing blogs and who has international experience, or do they need a strategic thinker with a proven track record of building marketing departments? Add to that a person's particular experience and ability to connect with the partners with whom they will work, and you start to see the wide variety of tradeoffs.

Skill set and experience provide the foundation, but chemistry is critical for success in the role. It's the quality of the personal relationship that the CMO has with senior leadership that will make a big difference in how much the firm gets out of its marketing efforts. Together the CMO and leadership should be able to frame goals, clarify messaging and discuss where the firm wants to be. It will help the CMO understand and map out a plan for how to spend time and money. Still, being effective is not easy. If a CMO wants a seat at the table, he or she needs to constantly add value.

2. *Needs Assessment:* Before beginning the search for a CMO, savvy firms will conduct a needs assessment. If done correctly, it will involve a broad swath of partners in considering where the CMO should focus. For example, if a firm has no plans to do client interviews, they may not need to hire someone who is a black-belt in qualitative primary research.

It is worthwhile to spend a small portion of the money allocated for the CMO search and recruitment to have a professional do an audit of the firm's needs. Have the recruiter or a consultant come in to survey several partners, those who will be most likely to work with the individual, as well as those who may be naysayers. Give serious consideration to who needs to have a voice in the process.

Once that is done, an accurate job description can be crafted and a search can begin. Not only will the likelihood of finding the right person increase, but the partners involved in the process will be more invested in the person hired.

According to Steven Spiess, the Chief Operating Officer at Brownstein Hyatt Farber Schreck, LLP, "One firm's business development and marketing leader is not another's and so people come in not being what the firm expects. It will also depend upon the maturity of the firm and how wide-ranging their geographic footprint. Are they a big law firm with a corporate and litigation department, or is it a firm with a single robust practice area? Where are they in their business cycle? Once the firm makes a decision to hire, they need to do a real soul-searching exercise and figure out what type of person they will need to help them do the job."

Steve continues, "The more specific and direct input the firm can provide, the better the search process will be." It is important that the soul searching as well as the interviewing process are not steps that involve just partners and shareholders. Steve believes, "The more inclusive you can be, involving staff within the marketing function and others who know how the business operates, the better position you will be in to attract the right person."

3. *Structure:* Another key to hiring the right person is the organizational and reporting structure. Sometimes the ideal reporting structure has the CMO reporting to an Executive Director but with a dotted line or exposure to the firm's chairman or another firm leader. Other times, it may mean reporting directly to the chairman or a marketing partner. When making the decision, consider the structure of the firm's administrative organization and to whom other directors report.

Also, consider the best way for this person to gain traction with partners and with other C-suite colleagues. If the Executive Director is knowledgeable about strategy and an inclusive leader who has a trusted relationship with their direct reports, it may make sense to have the CMO report directly to the Executive Director. However, if the Executive Director is not someone known for bringing the C-suite together or who lacks facilitation skills, it might not be the right reporting relationship.

Some CMOs say they will only take the job if they report directly to the Chair or senior-most partner at the firm. While this may sound correct at first blush, if the CMO reports to the Chair, he or she may become only identified with that one person. That can create a delicate situation and may turn out to be a recipe for failure. In either case, the CMO should be a part of the existing overall management team.

Despina Kartson, a CMO who has served successfully at large law firms with several different reporting relationships, says, "To be truly impactful, the CMO should have a proverbial seat at the table, having an opportunity to be involved and provide input when appropriate, in firm leadership meetings."

Still, all agree that it is vital for the CMO to have support-ive relationships with his or her colleagues and, whenever possible, report to the same person at least on a dotted-line basis. This allows all of the C-level professionals, such as the Chief Information Officer, Chief Knowledge Officer, and Chief Human Resource Officer, to engage and effectively work on joint projects together.

4. *Marketing Committees:* Law firm leaders often ask if they should have a marketing committee. Marketing committees can be beneficial structures to provide input to the CMO to allow him or her to know more about what is going on within the firm. They can also help facilitate projects by reporting back to the partner-ship and providing support for the department. The committee can be helpful when trying to coordinate the marketing efforts of a multi-office operation.

But not all marketing committees are equal. If they are com-posed without great thought, or composed of highly political indi-viduals, they can be deleterious to the firm's marketing efforts. It is essential that when forming these groups, attention be placed to ensure that they are staffed thoughtfully and that the committee's members have the firm's best interest at heart. Partners should not be added to the committee if their purpose is to push an agenda or ensure their rising profile as the reason for their involvement.

"The purpose of a marketing committee in a partnership environment should be to serve as a focus group for the CMO," says Jennifer Scalzi. "It's a way for the CMO to get a feel for internal/external reactions to plans and strategies, rather than to be dictated to about those plans and strategies."

5. *Miracles:* Don't expect miracles. Firm leadership should lay out exactly what they expect from the CMO role and communicate that clearly to the firm's partners as well as to the applicants. Be honest and don't oversell the job by calling it something it is not. The word "strategy" should not be placed in a title just to attract the highest-level candidate. The firm needs to be prepared to provide the resources (personnel and financial) to allow the new hire to get to where they want to be. Before making the hire, the firm should be comfortable answering questions regarding the department's annual budget and the processes for expense approval.

6. *Trust:* Before you make the hire, know that you will need to trust this person well enough to provide him or her access to crucial financial information, such as client realization, partner productivity and other strategic measures. Not only will the data be vital to the CMO's success, but without trust, his or her impact will be limited at best.

Trust is critical in this hire. The misalignment between expectations and reality is usually what leads to shorter tenures. As Jennifer points out, "Just like in life, firms and candidates want to be liked, and that can play out in the interview process. Unfortunately, when a firm doesn't fully recognize or disclose their 'warts,' final candidates are forced to take a leap of faith rather than make a highly informed decision. The same is true for candidates. If they aren't able to address areas where they see the potential for personal growth, a firm may end up with a professional who has reached their peak and doesn't believe he or she needs to grow or continue learning."

7. *Onboarding:* Create an onboarding program to get the individual acculturated into the firm quickly. Management leaders need to be supportive of the hire and be champions for inclusion.

Steve Spiess says, "I am a big believer in onboarding as it can make or break a person's impression. In their first four to six weeks, new CMOs should have breakfasts and dinners arranged with the management committee, department chairs, and other C-level executives. Within the first ninety days, they will need support from senior management to encourage these activities and give them the right exposure. If you have multiple offices, send the CMO to visit those offices. It's even better if they can make the trip with another chief or a COO who can personally introduce them to their new colleagues."

The onboarding process is key and will help form the overall impression your new hire has of the firm. It's all about setting up the new CMO to have the resources for success. Much of the attention should be spent on introductions and getting him or her to connect with those with whom he or she will work. The more connections you can facilitate between your new CMO and their colleagues and the partners, the better for the new hire, and the higher the dividend.

What Makes a CMO a Success?

The characteristics that lead one CMO to be more successful than the next vary firm to firm. At some firms, it may be important for the CMO to push the envelope and to cultivate new ideas, while at other firms it is more important for the individual to create and train a team to provide a service to the partnership. Success often depends on a good match between the CMO and the seat of power of the firm. One consistent success factor, however, is chemistry and the ability to work closely with the firm's leadership. If the CMO has a positive alignment with the power of the firm, together they can get a lot done.

The Fit Is Essential

Barry Wolf, Executive Partner at Weil Gotshal, says of the cultural fit, "I think the most important thing is the fit between the individual and the nature of the firm. Different firms have different atmospheres and ways of operation, and firm leaders need to understand their firm's culture and find someone who fits in. As for who the right individual is for the job, law firms are horizontal in their structure, not vertical corporations, and sometimes people who come from corporate America have different ideas."

"I think the most important thing is the fit between the individual and the nature of the firm. Different firms have different atmospheres and ways of operation, and firm leaders need to understand their firm's culture and find someone who fits in."

—**Barry M. Wolf,** Weil, Gotshal & Manges LLP

Barry continues, "Everyone at Weil can go to the CMO, and there is not a formal chain of command. Someone who is comfortable working with a horizontal organization is critical. That person can earn the respect of the partners, particularly if they are practical and understand the organization."

Robert Lennon, Chief Business Development & Communications Officer at Weil, admits that at times being a CMO can also be a self-effacing job, even though one needs to maintain the highest level of skill. "If the mundane things don't get done, the more strategic work doesn't matter. You need to think, 'How am I going to help them' versus, 'How am I going to teach or train them?' The pitch books have to get done and you need to keep track of whether or not a client wants their name on the cover."

Robert has made considerable strides at the firm, particularly in the area of best-in-class research. Conducting research on a prospective client and knowing what the company has done over the past few months and which law firms it uses for various practice areas has become second nature to Robert and his team. "We want to be able to update the partner with the very best data, in the shortest amount of time. By doing so, we can work with them on executing a strategy."

So yes, the role is one of being strategic and thinking about the big picture, but Robert and his team also understand that the most important value-add is for his group to service the ongoing new business-related needs of the firm's partners.

Robert's group has specific triggers in place, set up by using several different technologies and metrics so that partners are alerted if a meaningful business event or economic indicator takes place at a client or prospect company. It's not a one-stop set-up but rather a combination of external news data, layered with sophisticated internal data mining.

Communications and Leadership Skills Are Key

Leadership coach Natalie Loeb, of Loeb Leadership Development Group, believes that communication is one of the central tenets to a marketer's success. "Communication is everything," says Natalie. "It's impossible for a leader to overcommunicate, and CMOs need to feel comfortable communicating consistently with their messaging and doing this constantly with multiple parties. They need to be honest and candid. They need to share lessons, failures, and demonstrate vulnerability. Communications skills can make a huge difference in the success or failure of a CMO."

Natalie notes the importance of internal marketing as an area that even the very best marketers can overlook. "This is vital," says Natalie. "Being conscious of your internal customers is key. It's what will often make the difference between having the firm adopt good ideas versus having partners ask, 'What do all of these marketing people do?'"

Face-to-face contact is a must and makes a difference in any professional's success, but this is particularly true in marketing where there is a strong need to constantly prove oneself and convince others to do things they may feel uncomfortable doing.

Natalie says, "CMOs can ask great questions and should go on listening tours. They should take the time to build those relationships. Some CMOs don't want to impose on partners, but in truth, I think the partners are most impressed with those that pull their seat up to the table literally and figuratively. They want them to take the lead in many of the discussions. CMOs need to push the envelope."

CMOs need to have the ability to communicate within the partnership and to lead within their department. Jennifer Scalzi states, "People with true leadership skills are much harder to find than people who have solid business development or marketing skills. What you want is someone who matches the maturity of your organization, aligns with your values, and has had a track record of success across a variety of areas."

With all this in mind, it's not rare to find that the large law firms with multipronged programs pay a million dollars a year for an experienced CMO.

Staffing the Department

As a firm's practice becomes more sophisticated and the organizational chart becomes more complex, the firm may have staff members who focus exclusively on client surveys or social media function. Practice and industry-focus groups are now part of most multi-office law firms. Many firms now have practice group attorneys or marketers embedded within key departments. Regardless, most CMOs with whom I spoke prefer not to have more than seven direct reports, with four being optimal.

Henry Nassau of Dechert sees assigning people to practice groups as important, but only if they have a thorough understanding of what is taking place in the area. Speaking of the practice group manager who handles the marketing within his industry group, he says, "She has a true grasp on what the lawyers do at the firm. She is smart and lives and breathes the business. She will read the *Wall Street Journal* or the *Financial Times* on a daily basis and often say to partners, 'Did you see this? Does this impact your practice?'"

A good marketing team will be able to work seamlessly with lawyers who have varying skill sets and requirements. While some rainmakers will have specific ideas about how they will implement an initiative or advance a client relationship, others will want a more involved and proactive marketing team to help them with strategy and to offer ideas and locate opportunities.

CMOs should keep in mind that marketers at all levels need to know more than just the tactics they are being asked to implement. To operate effectively and develop professionally, they need to know the strategy and the decisions and reasoning behind that strategy. The best marketing organizations have leaders who communicate with their entire organization, not just to a select group of deputies.

Amanda Brady of Major Lindsey says, "If you educate your team on the organization's strategy and what keeps you as the CMO or managing partner up at night, they can be more responsive." Amanda suggests, "Give them the opportunity to offer different solutions to problems, and something more. Allow them to be invested in the outcome, and they will be invested in the organization. No one wants to work in a vacuum."

More firms are using client teams to organize their business development efforts. Many CMOs are involved in conducting or overseeing client satisfaction surveys. Newer technology allows CMOs to integrate enhanced customer relationship management (CRM) or Salesforce-like programs for data management, and social media is now an essential tactic for visibility. Firms may also use software like Foundation, a system that helps organize the firm's experiential information. Implementing these technologies frees up the marketing department to be able to handle even more significant and more sophisticated projects.

David Bernstein of Debevoise says, "As we now know, it takes a village to raise a child; it also takes a coordinated team to make rain." David's view of marketing is definitely one that sees how the marketing department can support the efforts of the partners in a service capacity.

Lawyers like David understand that a marketing team is critical. "Marketers can help identify prospective clients, research businesses and legal needs, and develop powerful and persuasive marketing materials. For a pitch, they can help pull together the increasingly detailed information required in RFP responses. But there is much more they can do even after the pitch. Whether the pitch is successful or not, the marketing team can interview the client to understand the strengths and weaknesses of our pitch."

David continues, "Marketing teams also can do much to help build the reputation of a group, which is necessary to support a rainmaker. The detailed submissions required to the many ranking organizations are critical and take a tremendous amount of time to do right — a good marketing group can play a critical role here. The marketing team can also help develop relationships with key media contacts so that the group's lawyers can regularly have the opportunity to comment on critical developments in the law. And they can help plan CLE programs for clients, which is another great way of building a reputation and promoting the group to clients and prospective clients."

The CMO of the Future

The CMO of the future will be able to do all of the things that have been mentioned here. They should be good managers, leaders, and communicators, and have strong chemistry with the firm's leaders. They should also understand technology and look at things from the client's perspective. With the proper resources in place and the support of the partnership, they can contribute to the growth of the business.

Reena SenGupta of RSG Consulting created and produces the *Financial Times* Innovative Law Firm Awards. "Smart CMOs in Europe have stopped marketing along legal practice area lines and are instead focused on the client or a topic/risk the client is absorbed in and facing. They have realized that as long as law firms are structured along the lines of their own products and services, they will remain focused on themselves and out of alignment with the client. A data strategy is critical and CMOs should be involved in formulating this with their CIOs and giving their lawyers a competitive edge through better knowledge management and sharing. There is an overlap between business development and knowledge management — and great marketers know how to fuse the two together to add value to clients and make compelling client communications."

Regarding how CMOs and other legal marketers can stay ahead of the curve, Charles Martin of Macfarlanes, says, "I think senior marketing people are in a very privileged and interesting place. My counsel to them would be to work very hard in three highly related ways."

"First, to understand the client world — the firm's clients, but also clients in general — what they want and what they feel about what they are not getting. You constantly hear from clients that there is an unarticulated and unsatisfied need out there. Marketers need profoundly to understand the needs of the clients. That should be the first objective."

"The second is to understand the whole firm and what capabilities make it unique, and how those capabilities differentiate it. Where its competitive advantage actually lies. Which, by the way, may be hard for partners at the coalface to see."

"The third area is to leverage the relationships senior marketing managers have with their counterparts in other law firms and other professional services firms to get valuable insights into what other people are doing. What ideas are out there that their firms should either adopt or have good reasons for not adopting."

Charles sums it up by saying, "If you explore all three of those strands, you will be in an extraordinarily powerful and valuable position to counsel partners and senior management on where the opportunities and risks for the firm lie."

Think Piece

Reforming the CMO Search to Target Turnover

By Jennifer Scalzi*

Strong marketing leadership is a prime area of opportunity to help firms navigate through what will prove to be a transformative chapter in the legal industry. The stakes are high, with expectations to match, and the abundance of data on CMO "churn" over the last decade illustrates what can happen when expectations and reality fail to intersect. While we've seen tenure numbers begin to climb, research and experience both point to the same issue: a disconnect between the process of hiring and then fully capitalizing on the talent of a chief marketing officer. Defy the statistics by setting the stage for progress from the very beginning.

Before the Interview Process

Decision Makers

The makeup of the hiring committee responsible for selecting a CMO will set the tone for the entire process. Managing partners, lawyers who are high-end users of Marketing, and HR directors all contribute valuable perspective, and could be even more effective when combined with the insight of a marketing insider. Without input from someone who understands the nuances of the marketing world, it can be difficult to spot the difference between a candidate who is excellent on paper and/or in person, but may lack the true

---

*   Jennifer Scalzi is the CEO of Calibrate Legal which works with its law firm clients to help them achieve optimal performance from their business services teams to drive top and bottom line impact. She can be reached at jennifer@calibrate-legal.com.

skill set that will take your firm forward. Placing trust and authority in a party that can speak both languages, whether an internal marketing ally or a recruiting partner, can ensure the voice of the marketer is represented in the decision-making process.

Playbook

The hiring committee's various backgrounds will, and should, influence their individual decisions. That diversity of opinion is a strength that can often bring challenges, as well. With that in mind, it's important to define your collective objectives early on in order to avoid wasting significant time and creating frustration in the months to follow. The expectations laid out in the job description should encompass the goals of the group, not the goals of an individual. Once the committee is able to get on the same figurative page in terms of their expectations and goals, they can move forward with direction and clarity. It's easier to identify your strongest candidates when you're working with consistent criteria. The alternative is a popularity contest, where subjective likeability and personal preference rule.

During the Interview Process

Your Brand

For better or worse, law firms and candidates both want to be liked. It's human instinct, but one that can prevent the most telling conversations from ever emerging during the interview process. The substance of those discussions can be the difference between a long-term CMO and another statistic. In the interest of being liked or respected, firms and professionals often skip the important work of identifying who they are (and are not), what they value, what they offer in the marketplace, and yes, where there is still room for improvement. Law firms and candidates alike each deserve and want to make a truly informed decision, and that calls for reciprocal candor. Get comfortable asking those difficult questions of yourself *and* the person on the other side of the table.

Indicators

There are certain indicators that separate the CMOs of the past and those of the future. Use your time with candidates to assess their knowledge of/experience with:

- Two or more full cycles of enterprise-wide change management
- Developing and implementing an enterprise-wide strategy with positive results
- Understanding the nuances of a marketing/BD team and optimal performance
- Fostering a business perspective beyond the legal industry
- Driving innovation in a professional services setting
- Adapting to a changing marketplace with skills that prove their ability to pivot when needed
- Breaking down internal silos, designing goals that align with the global picture
- Building partnerships for clients that will benefit them as a value-add and serve as a business development tool

In return, here are some of the questions firms should expect to hear from seasoned candidates looking to assess the viability of the position:

- What is the firm's financial position? Do you have debt outside of real estate assets?
- What is your compensation model?
- What succession plan is in place?

- When is the last time the firm performed a market positioning audit to understand the place it holds in the competitive landscape?

- What value-add offerings do you currently use to attract prospective clients?

- What is the firm's threshold for innovation/risk?

- Does the firm currently hold any key strategic partnerships?

After the Interview Process

Preparation

Spend the interim time between the CMO's acceptance and start date wisely. Assemble as much information and background as possible on the state of marketing and client experience within your firm. This groundwork, coupled with the original expectations agreed upon by your hiring committee, can provide the new CMO with the resources needed to shorten the learning curve and get to work. Another option is to dispatch an operational analyst to provide the new CMO with an independent inventory of department offerings, systems, processes, and data. That information will provide the CMO with a roadmap of department-wide resources, enabling him or her to target potential areas of improvement and begin building a culture of measurement and accountability within the team.

The initial days, weeks and months after a CMO's arrival are a formative time and it is important to exercise patience as he or she comes up to speed. Given the highly personal nature of marketing, it takes a CMO some time to begin truly understanding the firm's culture and how to thrive within it. Once they do, you should expect and encourage them to foster the kind of environment that will cultivate the kind of forward thinking that will take your firm into the future by prioritizing:

- R&D and market intelligence to drive industry offerings
- Proactive business planning and reporting using Account Based Marketing
- Idea generation to create innovation in service delivery
- Cross-collaboration with other business services teams across your firm

If done correctly, the marketing team can actually pay for itself by enabling your lawyer sales force to operate at their highest and best throughout the course of the sales funnel process.

Marketing is the place where the internal and external needs of your firm collide, and it will be a driving force in law firm sustainability in the years to come. The right CMO in your firm will be a cornerstone for a successful strategy in this increasingly client-driven marketplace, where firms are hungry for competitive advantages that truly differentiate them in ways that will help engage potential clients in lasting partnerships. To capitalize on this investment, law firms need to be intentional and formulaic in their approach to bridge the gap between finding and *keeping* the right leader.

Chapter 6

Rewarding Business Development, Coaching and Training

A constant refrain I hear from law firm leaders is that their partners fall into two camps: those who are outstanding at developing business, and the others, who "just don't get it." I have heard lots of reasons for this: Certain lawyers "don't have the marketing gene." Others are "young and haven't grown into the role," or the partner's practice "is just a *really* difficult area to market." And very often, the business development-challenged partners I've met fall into one of three archetypes.

The first is the partner I call the Tasmanian devil. He is the one who by his own initiative speaks at numerous conferences and also writes lengthy articles for various legal publications on a wide range of unrelated topics. The Tasmanian devil is always involved in activities that feel like marketing and will show up for any networking event where his presence is requested; however, when asked about the new business he expects to bring in, he responds, "These things may take years." Still, years pass and he has few results to show for his activity. He is a regular customer of the marketing and business development department, requesting materials to support his speaking engagements or help in getting bylined article reprint permissions, but he rejects any feedback on the effectiveness of his marketing. His boundless energy, enthusiasm, and activity show little return on the firm's investment or the personal time he spends on marketing.

Then there is the data scientist. This lawyer is a cousin of the Tasmanian devil, in that she spends a lot of time on marketing, but her focus is on data points. She often requests reams of information from the marketing department, but also calls on the finance department to supply her with the same statistics. She then will contact the firm's library staff for additional background resources. The data scientist prefers not to meet potential clients face to face, but she believes that by studying the information, she may come across some hidden secret to marketing. She is willing to send out lots of client alerts and mailings, because she believes that this is the way she should market her work. Still, she is more concerned with spending her time analyzing the reports and weighing her options than going out to meet with other human beings, and asking them for business.

Lastly, there is the partner I call the snowman. This is the partner who has great talent and capability, and may even have a good book of business, but he is frozen when it comes to extending himself. He does not want to introduce other partners to his contacts and he is uncomfortable meeting with potential clients. The snowman prefers not to promote himself in terms of speaking engagements or networking unless absolutely forced. He says he finds marketing distasteful and often tells people, "that isn't why I went to law school."

But all is not lost for the Tasmanian devil, the data scientist or the snowman.

There are ways to train all three of these archetypes to market, though at the core each one needs to be motivated by both the firm's compensation structure and assisted by being provided with the skills to do so. And while there isn't a one-size-fits-all approach to motivation and skill, there are steps that firms can take that are proven to make a difference.

Providing four things to partners is essential:

1. A compensation structure that supports a culture of business development, collaboration and mentorships;

2. A culture that rewards best behaviors, supports planning and encourages business development;

3. A program for access to training and coaching to support the efforts and provide the tools to those who are in need;

4. An operations and marketing process, to help support the process of developing business.

Compensation

There are hundreds of studies showing the causal relationship tying compensation to performance in the workplace. The general premise is that by holding out a carrot, you get the type of performance you hope to achieve. While the simplicity of this equation might work when training bunnies, human beings are far more complicated. In fact, studies show that in some cases, misguided incentive-based compensation programs can actually work as a factor against performance. Unless the compensation is carefully tied directly to the very specific performance the firm wants to reward, and the cultural conditions to support the behavior are in place, these structures can backfire.

A great example of this can be seen even more clearly in the retail arena. When a local department store in New York City recently changed its compensation system to reward salespeople solely on their sales (not on collaboration or customer service), many shoppers started to avoid the place like the plague. Why? It was not that the selection of items or pricing model had changed, but rather that now customers felt constantly accosted by salespeople tripping over one another to say, "May I help you? May I help you?" While in and of itself asking customers if they need help is not a bad practice, in this case customers were also overhearing salespeople arguing over who approached the customer first. And if a customer happened to ask a salesperson other than the one who had initially helped them if, for example, they had a particular size, the response would be a snarky, "I'm not your salesperson!"

Think about a law firm where origination is the only thing that is prized and collaboration with other partners is not rewarded. These are the circumstances where secrecy is fostered, a lack of peer-to-peer communication exists, and you see more partner departures due to the absence of cultural adhesion. This can also result in multiple partners pitching a single client, or worse, a client who may already be a client of the firm being approached by a separate practice (yes, it happens). When it comes to business development, partners will be expected to sink or swim on their own. And though the firm's management may say they prize collaboration — even having guest speakers talk about the subject and using all of the right buzzwords — do they really? Will a client get the best work and the right business solutions from the firm when the partners are not rewarded for turning to one another to problem solve?

If the compensation system's incentives are not set up properly, it may reward the wrong type of behavior, or create a department store type of competition that is unwieldy and destructive. Many firms today seem to be very much eat-what-you-kill, with lateral partners moving in and out of their firms lured by the sparkle of a royal starting bonus.

A sharing or more collaborative form of lockstep compensation, where partners are paid based on seniority within the organization, not by what business they originate, can help partners view their own firm as a more collegial place. Partners chant in unison, "a rising tide lifts all ships." However, even a lockstep system can have its challenges. What happens when those who are not quite glued to the firm become more ambitious or others begin to feel they are not rewarded for working harder or bringing in more clients? In addition, what about the young partner who quips about an older partner who has taken on more of the firm's management responsibilities and complains that the older one isn't pulling his or her weight. Lockstep can work well, but only if the culture and leadership is there to support it.

A compensation system should be used as a tool to reward the behaviors a firm wants to encourage and those that will help with business development. It should also be transparent to exhibit fairness. Something between eat/kill and lockstep seems right for most firms: a compensation system that encourages both business development and collaboration.

When firm leaders think about the compensation structure, they should consider starting by thinking in terms of their clients. What does the client want and what does the client value?

On the fairness issue, Barry Wolf at Weil Gotshal points out, "Money is one aspect, but the relative ranking of where a partner appears is also important." Weil has a system that is extremely transparent. "It not only shows the compensation that other partners are earning, but it shows where each partner is on the list relative to one another. That allows us to send messages as to what we value."

At Weil, each year during compensation season, the partners are asked to respond to five questions. Two of the questions focus on collaboration: "Which partners helped you the most?" and "Who did you help?" These questions help the firm leadership relay to partners that people who collaborate will be rewarded.

Firm Culture

While the compensation system is the keystone of making a business development culture work, beyond the paycheck there are many ways a firm can support and incentivize business development. Firm leaders, from the chairperson to a department or practice head, need to ensure that they provide psychic kudos to those who collaborate, mentor and, in general, play nicely in the new business sandbox. Whether it means spotlighting new business wins when they involve a team effort or highlighting the collaborative work taking place for one of the firm's top clients, recognition plays a big part in demonstrating to the partners that this behavior really matters.

There are lots of formal ways to do this as well. Partner meetings are a great forum for communicating valuable messages. If the partners meet regularly, leadership can ensure that at each meeting there is a discussion of business development. One managing partner I know ensures that each time the full partnership meets, he has something to say regarding new business. It is always an item on the agenda. The managing partner mentions significant wins that transpired since the last meeting and asks the partners who played a role to present a mini case study as to how the business was brought in. As people tend to remember stories, presenting these case studies at a firm meeting rewards the partners who were involved and reinforces the firm's values. Firm newsletters and other communications to the partnership can also support these messages.

And remember all of those things your mother taught you. Informally congratulating someone simply by visiting the person in his or her office or thanking people in front a group goes a long way in showing you appreciate their efforts.

Business Development Training and Coaching

Training

In working with newly launched law firms, one of the first things I typically recommend is that they spend their marketing dollars on business development training and coaching. Business development training is popular with both associates and partners, and for good reason. Not only does training provide tools to lawyers for developing new business, but simply the firm's act of providing training sends a message to lawyers that it cares enough to invest in them.

When it comes to newly minted lawyers, most are aware that large firms typically provide associates access to business development training. (These days, the absence of such training can be seen as a mark against the firm.) In addition, practice is necessary to develop skills, so it is beneficial to start associates on developing these skills early in their careers. Also keep in mind that some of the best client relationships may be formed when lawyers are on the lowest rung of their organization's ladder. Having the years to develop those relationships can pay off when the young client moves into a position to make hiring decisions.

There are many wonderful law firms whose management would rather have associates simply focus on doing legal work, but new business training need not be exclusively in the domain of partners. Many of the skills involved in new business training — such as establishing empathy, putting oneself in the client's shoes — can be helpful even if the associate is never in a position to ask for new business.

Often firms will give associates a nominal budget to entertain clients or prospects, or at a minimum, make it easier to expense these costs. It sends a message to associates that they are part of the business team and their relationship-building skills are valued. The hope is that some associates will stay to become partners at the firm, but even if they leave, that they will remain grateful that this important education was part of their training.

New partners, if they've not yet been trained, should be trained as soon as possible. You may make more of an investment to train or coach your high-potential lawyers, but training is applicable to most lawyers. Yolanda Cartusciello of PP&C Consulting says, "I am a big believer in training. Not every lawyer will be a rainmaker, but they may be a rain barrel carrier. As a coach, I try to get the lawyer to expand his or her knowledge as to the client's needs. We want our coaches to think, 'How can I be helpful to these people?' You need to give before you get."

Darryl Cross, author of *Cultivating Excellence: The Art, Science, and Grit of High Performance in Business,*[1] is a performance futurist and certified team performance coach who focuses on the fusion of teams, technology and training. In writing his book, he combined primary and secondary research and spoke with many high-performing individuals, including top athletes, police officers, and Navy SEALs. People in these professions who did not perform would face, as Darryl puts it, "terminal consequences."

"When equal competitors work as a team, there is a sense of internal competition and sharing best practices, collaboration, and fear of letting each other down."

—Darryl Cross, author of *Cultivating Excellence: The Art, Science, and Grit of High Performance in Business*

From his findings, Darryl does not believe that compensation is the key motivating factor. "What matters most is to encourage these people by having them work as teams," says Darryl. He believes that training that takes place as a team works best. "Teams make a big difference. When equal competitors work as a team, there is a sense of internal competition and sharing best practices, collaboration, and fear of letting each other down. The biggest detriment we have at law firms is the emphasis of a cult of the individual versus a culture of collaboration, and no other profession where performance really matters — musicians, astronauts, and the like — works that way. Even as team members, astronauts and Navy SEALs compete

---

1.   River Grove Books (2017).

against one another and they each improve. If you put colleagues on teams together, they work together and each member improves their performance. The team does as well."

Darryl's team premise does make sense. After all, when you have a multifaceted deal, you get your best people to work together to get it done, but often when it comes to business development, we reward people for developing the matter as individuals and producing the results separately. Teams, especially diverse ones, generally get better results on new business pitches.

Traditionally, one-on-one coaching was typically where lawyers receive the most valuable input on their business development efforts, while also providing a safe environment for lawyers to practice their new skills and address their shortcomings. Nevertheless, there are trainers who supplement the individual coaching with small-team coaching using an experiential element. Consultant Susan Saltonstall Duncan of RainMaking Oasis, LLC generally trains partners in groups of five to ten over a period of six to nine months, usually bringing them together four times during the program. "In between the sessions, I ask them to complete some homework and put into practice some of the concepts covered in each session. In one firm, the lawyers have to create a business plan and they develop the plan as we work together, incorporating ideas from the workshops as well as the one-on-one coaching I provide." This group coaching is supplemented with six months of individual, customized coaching for mid-level partners who already are developing business. The teams of partners selected for the groups most often represent different practices and offices so that partners can actively collaborate and start cross-selling during the coaching program.

The same team principle is at work at firms across the country as they focus on existing clients and client team management. By doing so, they shift their thinking from the work that an individual partner is doing for a client to the work that the firm is doing for the client across-the-board. Client teams are going full steam ahead at many large firms. These teams help ensure that a multidisciplinary approach is being taken to focus on the client in a holistic way, supporting the training that partners are receiving.

Coaching

There is a difference between training and coaching. Traditional training is generally presented by one trainer to many participants, and generally, less personalized than one-on-one type of coaching. It is usually held in a more formal setting in which the trainer provides tips and approaches to developing business. Coaching usually refers to an activity that falls within the domain of training but is more individualistic and generally conducted on a one-on-one basis.

Coaching is about understanding a lawyer's practice and how he or she can grow it. If done properly, a lot of time is spent listening to the lawyer. A good coach will take into account the lawyer's practice, clients, competition, and personality. Coaching generally takes place over a series of meetings and isn't a one-shot deal.

Not only does coaching help for its instructional benefits, it helps keep the client — the lawyer — on track in terms of accountability. When a lawyer knows they have an appointment with a coach, they usually work toward that goal. It's the concept of the student who knows that the piano teacher is coming in the afternoon, so they need to start practicing in the morning.

Coaches will usually assign homework, whether it's a practice run of taking a fellow partner to lunch and talking about the business or having a more serious meeting with a potential client or referral source.

While in-firm business development executives can certainly provide coaching, and many have the skill sets to do so, often the most effective coaches are outsiders brought in to focus on an individual lawyer. The outsider will be in a better position to speak frankly to the lawyer and provide honest feedback that may be harder for a business development staffer to impart. Coaching is not something that should be conducted by another partner; in fact, the best rainmakers are not necessarily the best coaches.

A good coach will help provide guidance to the lawyer that he or she may need just to get jumpstarted. Consultant Tim Corcoran of Corcoran Consulting Group, LLC, says, "Lawyers are fantastic at figuring out how to maximize their success when they are given a road map."

Who are the best coaches? It depends. While experience is key, chemistry and trust are even more important. Some CMOs give their partners the chance to interview two or three different coaches before hiring one with whom to work. Not only does that take into account the partner's personality and preference for working style, but it also gets them invested in the coaching process early on.

According to Silvia Coulter, a LawVision principal consultant, co-founder of LSSO, the Legal Services and Sales Organization, and a former Fortune 50 sales executive, "In order to coach the best, you have had to have walked in their shoes. Most great sales coaches are not lawyers, but they have been in sales. When you know what these people are facing and understand it is a win/lose situation, you have more credibility."

Once hired, a coach will work closely with the firm's CMO to understand the culture and the systems in place to support the partner. While the engagements should take place within a framework of confidentiality, the consultant may want to suggest certain systemic changes that need to be made to the firm in order for business development to thrive.

Operations and Processes

We've all seen the practice groups where people work well together. Partners meet regularly and associates feel integral to the business. Part of that comes from the ability to create an esprit de corps and to enjoy working as a team. Not only are these generally the most interesting people with whom to work, they are also usually the most successful.

According to Darryl Cross, if a runner competes in a 5K and wants to improve her time, she may start running with a friend, which will likely help her results. That natural reflex to push oneself to compete with others can be used for helping lawyers. As Darryl's research has shown, reliance on others brings out the three key components that set high performers apart from those with high potential: engaging in deliberate practice, leveraging managed competition, and participating in dynamic simulations of the real thing. Even if lawyers are doing well at developing business, the question is, how can you get them to do even better? This is just one reason that business development teams — collections of partners with diverse backgrounds, perspectives, and skill sets that come together as a practice along with their business development staff — are useful. It creates an atmosphere where people self-manage and seek to do their best every day.

Practice group leadership is important. There should be a clear definition of the group leader's tasks and responsibilities. Based on the particular firm's governance, these leaders should be held accountable in terms of business development. They should report in regularly to the department head or firm chair, yet have the flexibility to manage and encourage marketing as they see fit.

Practice leaders should be solid managers, but they may not need to be those with the best rainmaking skills. In fact, Tim Corcoran suggests, "If we put the top rainmakers in charge of a group, we may be making a mistake. If they are going to get calls, they might not share."

When marketing departments are given appropriate budgets, they can do great work to support partners. In general, marketing departments are getting better at tracking pitches, win/loss ratios, and which partners and practice groups win pitches and why. This information is vital. By tracking these activities and feeding the statistics back into the partnership, they provide the metrics for partners to see what other partners in the firm are doing and the impact of those activities. In addition, these metrics help the business development team locate patterns that will allow them to make appropriate investment recommendations. For example, if the firm is spending a lot of time responding to RFPs and only getting a 2% return rate, maybe they are responding to too many without having a stronger go/no go policy. They can also track statistics to tell how much work is coming in from alumni, from other law firms or from current clients who are referring business back to the firm. By reporting back on these statistics, it helps provide another psychic reward for the partners who are pursuing new business while holding the entire partnership accountable. At many firms, the marketing departments share weekly and monthly reports, showing the pitch activity and the year-to-date figures.

So while coaching and training can certainly support the growth of a lawyer's business development skill, the attention placed on such programs should be seen in context of a firm-wide system that supports these efforts.

Think Piece

Five Ways to Improve the ROI of Business Development

By Timothy B. Corcoran*

Law firms can be profoundly inefficient at business development. There are three common root causes: the partners tend to pursue what makes them comfortable; there are few metrics employed to measure what's effective; and there are minimal penalties for ineffective business development. The net result is that many law firms allow partners to engage in a high volume of "random acts of marketing" in the hope that, sooner or later, something will work. This approach, called "unconscious incompetence" in the psychology of learning, works because of the sheer volume of effort put forth. But that effort comes at a high cost.

Professional legal marketers often know how inefficient partner business development efforts can be, but are constrained from taking corrective action. This "conscious incompetence" can be caused by the traditional law firm power structure that tends to ascribe a higher value to partner preferences over the objective feedback of experts. There is never enough time in the day for legal marketers to handle the high volume of misguided ideas partners generate. This leaves little time for proactive guidance and thoughtful planning.

---

*   Timothy B. Corcoran is principal of Corcoran Consulting Group, LLC, a Trustee and Fellow of the College of Law Practice Management and was 2014 president of the International Legal Marketing Association. A former CEO, he advises law firm and law department leaders through the profitable disruption of outdated business models. Based in New York with a global client base, he authors *Corcoran's Business of Law* blog. tim@bringintim.com.

To break the cycle of inefficiency, here are five concrete ideas to improve the efficiency of law firm business development efforts.

1.   Follow the money. In every law firm, there are multiple practice groups offering multiple matter types, and for each matter type there are numerous tasks. The market values these services differently, and for each the firm generates variable profits. Rather than allocate to every partner a pro rata portion of the firm's marketing resources, firm leaders should allocate investment based in large part on financial criteria. This might mean a low-rate practice would receive less of the marketing budget than a high-rate practice. But profit matters, so a low-rate practice that has embraced project management and process improvement to boost profits might deserve more of the marketing budget. And a high-rate practice led by an expensive rainmaker with a large and expensive team might deserve fewer marketing resources until it re-engineers its offerings to improve profits.

The analysis doesn't have to be exhaustive to begin to prioritize. Practices and matters reflecting the firm's unique competitive differentiation and generating healthy profits should receive more marketing support than undifferentiated practices led by partners who aren't busy. These data provide support to firm leaders who are learning to say "no" to bad ideas.

2.   Embrace accountability. Few law firms have a strategic plan that's useful to guide day-to-day operational decisions. And many practice and individual marketing plans collect dust until compensation review time. Often, even robust marketing plans erroneously focus more on activity volume and tactics than on effectiveness. There's a simple litmus test: if the marketing plan links specific actions to specific financial goals, it has the ingredients for accountability. Without financial goals, it's really just a list of tactics that may or may not produce results. ROI, or return on investment, is a relative measure. If a practice group spends $100K on a marketing campaign that leads to $250K in fees, this is good. When that same $100K invested in a more compelling initiative would have led to

$500K in fees, then the ROI is poor by comparison. Everyone must not only hold themselves accountable to engaging in activities that can produce measurable results, they must also acknowledge when their pet campaign deprives a more lucrative initiative of necessary investment. A little healthy competition is good to ensure only the best ideas earn the limited marketing investment.

3.   Publish scorecards. Law firms are competitive environments filled largely with competitive people, a situation well-suited for creating a culture of accountability. One way to improve accountability is to publish metrics. The goal isn't to criticize under-performance; it's to celebrate over-performance. For example, the marketing team might compile a scorecard ranking the relative effectiveness of the practice groups' proposals or RFP responses. There are best practices to improve the "win rate," such as by declining pitches with little chance of success, or starting a pitch process early enough to allow multiple edits rather than a last-second rush to beat the deadline. The scorecard provides a bit of a competitive edge and prompts the question, "How can we improve our effectiveness?"

Another example is to highlight success stories in internal communications. Instead of focusing solely on the results ("We won at trial!" or "We earned a spot on the preferred panel!"), focus on how the success was achieved. What tactics, teamwork, tools, processes, timeline, planning, etc., were instrumental in obtaining the positive result? By highlighting what is effective, it catches people doing things right, and gives everyone an approach to emulate.

4.   Reward activity and results. Most law firm compensation plans in some way reward the results of business development efforts. However, focusing solely on results can perversely discourage some lawyers from engaging in BD. Excellent rainmakers know they will earn steady rewards. But infrequent or novice business developers need to put forth far more effort, and this detracts from time earning rewards and recognition in their comfort zone, such as by billing working attorney time. Even when business development time is rewarded, the reward often lags the activities by such a long duration that the lawyer has to choose to earn less this year in return for potentially earning more next year. For risk-averse lawyers, the choice is often to avoid business development activities. Firms paying for BD activity don't just dole out cash for every lunch with a law school chum. Rather, rewards are generated by pursuing activities specifically identified in the marketing plan and linked to specific financial outcomes. Done well, a marketing plan identifies desirable outcomes and specific actions that generate these outcomes, and it provides lawyers with short- and long-term incentives to engage in the pursuit. On balance, compensation plans should offer more rewards for results than actions, but there's a lot of flexibility and room for identifying and rewarding actions that lead to results.

5.   It takes a village. Finally, one way to improve the effectiveness of lawyer business development is to stop asking lawyers to step too far away from their comfort zone. Consider the technical expert lawyer who prefers to sit at his desk all day toiling diligently on his colleagues' client files. Asking this lawyer to stop working and attend "Rainmaker 101" class deprives the firm of an expert billing healthy rates on critical files and demotivates the lawyer who's asked to pursue actions that are simply too great a stretch. Or consider the rainmaker with a $5M book of business who could easily grow the book to $8M, but who's required to return to the office and bill time because the compensation plan has an artificial requirement for both origination and production.

High-performing teams are comprised of different players with different roles and skills. This is true in sports, in business, and in law firms. Efficient firms might rely on a rainmaker to create an opportunity, but rely on the engaging and inquisitive partner adept at unearthing client's concerns to qualify and advance the opportunity. The technical expert might help craft a custom solution and project plan, while the partner who excels at matter management creates a budget and staffing plan, and some combination of the team coordinates on a presentation at the pitch meeting. This approach maximizes every partner's potential contribution rather than expects partners to do everything well.

Law firm leaders who wish to maximize their return on investment, who want to generate new, profitable revenue streams from new and existing clients, and who wish to foster a culture built on thoughtful analysis rather than whimsy will benefit from incorporating these ideas into each practice.

Chapter 7

Personal Positioning, Visibility and Tactics

Positioning

Ted Wells, David Boies, Evan Chesler and Mary Jo White. To anyone in the legal profession, these are household names. If a general counsel asks for an expert recommendation, or a law student searches online for a list of the country's best lawyers, these law firm partners are recognized as leading litigators. Interestingly, you may not even remember which firms they call home, proving the fact that their individual reputations go beyond law firm branding. They are supported by their own brand-name recognition. (In this case, these legal stars are with wonderful firms. Ted Wells is with Paul Weiss; David Boies, Boies Schiller; Evan Chesler, Cravath; and Mary Jo White, Debevoise.)

But what makes them such recognizable names with positive associations? For some, it's a successful career of dedicated government service, for others it's for trying near-impossible cases, mastering complex facts and winning significant victories. For most, it's that throughout their careers, they have spoken at relevant forums, authored articles and white papers, and talked with reporters.

For most lawyers surrounded by that magical aura of excellence, there is a backstory grounded on genuine legal skill. Chances are many of these lawyers had terrific mentors as they came up in the ranks, but to a person, they each studied and worked diligently to master their craft. They were the ones who as associates were burning the midnight oil and aiming for perfection. It may have been easier if there was a shortcut, but raising one's visibility while lacking the solid foundation that comes from doing great work doesn't succeed in the long run. Eventually, those folks are found out.

I was brought up hearing the rhyme, "Good better best, never let it rest, until the good is better and the better is the best." To me, that meant that one should always try to do the finest work possible. While I still think that should be one's focus, in order to market yourself in the legal profession it's essential to do more than just good work. But where does a lawyer start in positioning herself and building a reputation?

Research demonstrates that it takes significant time as well as natural ability to be known as a great anything. To hold a particular position in someone's mind, there usually need to be multiple and consistent impressions, meaning someone has heard your name or heard about your work multiple times. Maybe they've met you in person or they've read about you in a news article. But hopefully each time they've come across you or your name, they've had a positive association.[1]

Internal Reputations

Once an attorney has achieved that level of excellence, where does he or she start to build that positive association or reputation?

Sally Feldman, the CMO at Skadden, Arps, Slate, Meagher & Flom LLP, says, "Doing excellent work for clients is a prerequisite, as is a commitment to prioritizing the client's — and the firm's —

---

1. *See* Al Ries & Jack Trout, Positioning: The Battle for Your Mind (McGraw-Hill Education 2001).

best interests over a desire for recognition. That said, colleagues are often the best referral sources and internal profile-raising is key."

Sally is on the mark. If you are a lawyer in a law firm, the impression you create among partners, associates, and staff is vitally important. When your partners hear your name and associate it with a particular expertise — "she does great intellectual property work for tech companies" — they will be more likely to mention your name outside of the firm. They will tell their clients about you and consider you for new business opportunities. While law firm partners may feel that it is silly to think in terms of selling themselves internally to their partners — that their partners already know precisely what they do — they are often wrong. In this age of lateral movement and so much work on each person's plate, there is a need to reinforce your personal message over and over again. Even if a partner has been at a firm for many years, it is vital for her to consider her internal audience just as seriously as she would the external one.

When a partner laterals into a new firm, I suggest that he think about the internal roadshow he will create for his new colleagues. The CMO and lateral partner can work together on how to communicate the partner's practice and the ways he or she can help other firm partners and their clients by providing them with legal advice, business intelligence and connections. Doing this work internally at one's firm also provides a test case of sorts for the partner to try out ideas and establish his or her key selling attributes.

On a more macro level, sharing this information is more likely to create a collaborative environment; in a business where partners best serve their clients by drawing from the firm's full resources, they need to have a grasp of what their fellow partners are doing. In addition to benefitting marketing, there is an organizational byproduct of communicating this way. It helps reinforce a team-based culture.

David Burgess, the Publishing Director of the *Legal 500*, has a bird's-eye view of how law firm partners create both good and bad reputations, both within their own firms and externally throughout the legal community. To develop their rankings, the *Legal 500* interviews general counsel as well as hundreds of lawyers at law firms to gauge which lawyers are considered leading lawyers in specific areas of practice. "Some lawyers are well regarded by their partners but not by clients, and then there are the partners who clients like working with, but they are disliked back at the firm. The likability factor in building a reputation is key," he says.

While clients want to work with lawyers they like, the same is true of marketing people. David advises partners, "Be good to your marketing staff. Not only do they often have input into firm rankings, but they are also a key part of your business. When you don't treat them with respect, it's soul-crushing to them. The CMOs are an incredibly talented, smart and dedicated bunch. If you are good to them, they will go to the mat to help you, time and time again." Reputation is built both by being a great lawyer but also by being a decent person.

Focus

For most partners in a law firm, the days of being an excellent, well-rounded generalist lawyer are in the distant past, and a strong effort by general counsel to hire lawyers with specific expertise has been underway for years. While most firms have moved in this direction, and even the smallest firms today have an idea of their positioning, it is somewhat tougher for the individual practitioner. Having a focus and knowing the few things that you do well is a must in capturing a position in the marketplace.

Jamie Diaferia, a counselor to professional service firms on media, litigation and crisis strategy and CEO of Infinite Global Consulting Ltd., advises young lawyers, "First, develop a niche." Jamie points out, "Many lawyers tend to shy away from specialization, scared they will be pigeon-holed. But deep expertise in a niche area can help you stand out. And understand that how you work with clients — your personality, energy, and approach — is as important as what you do for them."

A great example of a firm with a solid focus is Wilkinson Walsh & Eskovitz, a young partnership run by veteran superstar litigators, Beth Wilkinson, Alex Walsh and Sean Eskovitz. Beth and Alex met after each had achieved illustrious careers and were both partners at Paul Weiss. Beth notably served as lead prosecutor of the Oklahoma City bombing case and later as General Counsel of Fannie Mae. Alex, after a career of public service that included clerking for U.S. Supreme Court Justice Stephen Breyer, had as her first private practice case to defend former White House aide I. Lewis "Scooter" Libby in a high-profile trial that involved charges of perjury and obstruction of justice in connection with the outing of a CIA agent. Sean Eskovitz, a former Assistant U.S. Attorney for the Southern District of New York, was a partner with Munger, Tolles & Olson LLP.

"Everything we do is designed to win trials. We recruit a diverse and talented group of lawyers. The values that we are trying to cultivate are eventually those things that will bring clients the results they want."

—Alexandra Walsh, Wilkinson Walsh & Eskovitz

Wilkinson Walsh & Eskovitz is focused solely on one thing: "winning high-stakes trials." This singular goal is stated prominently on their website. They have differentiated themselves by their work and their results for clients such as Pfizer and Philip Morris. Differentiation needs to go beyond marketing efforts by speaking about and demonstrating expertise.

While Wilkinson Walsh & Eskovitz handles just about all aspects of litigation, they have a clear and definitive idea of what they do best. "Storytelling comes from experience and taking a complex set of facts and finding the essence of what will be persuasive to a jury," says Beth. "It's not what you think is important. It's what the audience, the jury or the judge, cares about. It means reorienting the goal."

Alex points out that the way the firm recruits and trains its lawyers works in support of the firm's goals. "Everything we do is designed to win trials. We recruit a diverse and talented group of lawyers. The values that we are trying to cultivate are eventually those things that will bring clients the results they want."

In developing a niche, lawyers need to ask themselves what they want to be spending their time doing and what types of clients they want to attract. What industries are impacted and what are the problems that they want to help address? Then they need to ask themselves what they bring to the table that makes them different from the competition and how they add value. In many ways, this is a concept taken from product marketing. Product marketers will tell you not to look at a product's attributes (for the legal profession, that would be like saying "the lawyer is intelligent and has done a lot of litigation"), but rather its benefits ("the lawyer has helped many in the consumer-product arena mitigate their shareholder class action work"). To lawyers, I would say, consider what it is that you do for clients that helps them. Rather than being recognized as a real estate lawyer, wouldn't you rather be known as a lawyer who works with clients to solve their stickiest commercial real estate issues?

For both internal and external audiences, the lawyer should be able to identify specifics about her practice that set her apart. Sally Feldman says lawyers ask themselves, "Have I handled a string of particularly innovative transactions? Developed an uncommon or niche practice? Am I counsel of record to multiple Fortune 500 companies or several within a specific industry?" Sally remarks, "Characterizing their practice in a way that significantly narrows the peer group with whom they may compete for business is an important component of successful attorney marketing. And, of course, being able to convey what sets them apart is crucial, as is engaging in marketing activities geared toward a targeted audience of individuals responsible for hiring outside counsel and those with whom they consult."

To have an impact and break through the marketing clutter created by a populated profession, lawyers need to take a step back and ask themselves, "What do I do differently than others in this area, and is there anything that I can offer that is better, faster, more efficient or more sophisticated?" In essence, just like any product offering, a service offering needs to be differentiated before it is marketed. Only by distinguishing yourself from the rest of the pack, can you truly stand out.

Andrew Stamelman of Sherman Wells Sylvester & Stamelman LLP says that he was always acutely aware of how lawyers positioned themselves in the legal marketplace, but even more so when he joined with a few partners from his former firm to start their own law partnership. "We realized early on that you can't just show up and introduce yourself as a great tax lawyer or a great M&A lawyer. You need to specialize in an area; for me, that means taking exceptional care of family businesses and middle-market companies. Do something where you can be unique in your practice and make a distinguishable difference for clients," he says. Andrew mentors his younger partners and associates on the topic of differentiation, advising them about what they need to do to distinguish themselves, most importantly by doing outstanding work and mastering a targeted set of skills.

Tactics

Lawyers who are eager to make a name for themselves often jump into the pool of marketing only to reach haphazardly for any lifejacket. There may be the speaking engagement, quote in the *Wall Street Journal* or brand new blog, and the lawyer often wants to reach for all of them without considering what makes sense for his specific practice, abilities and the intended audience. While the decision can be highly nuanced, there are several approaches that can be utilized to increase a lawyer's profile.

Ralph Ferrara of Proskauer believes in a broad-brush yet thoughtful approach. Ralph says, "You have to do the things that will elevate your name and reputation in the legal community but you need to do it with a focus on the core competency that a prospective class of clients wants. Things like preparing a treatise in your core field, achieving bar recognitions and chairing various committees. No one today is driven to hire a firm solely on the reputation of the firm, or even a long relationship with a firm over decades." According to Ralph, "Potential clients are more interested in knowing your specific expertise and what was the last case you handled 'just like mine' and what was the result."

Public Speaking

Targeted speaking engagements are one of the best approaches to building a professional reputation. While a good marketing person can help ferret out the right industry conference, practice- or geography-related program at which a partner should speak, quite often conference organizers approach the firm. Before accepting an invitation to speak, consider: Is this a reputable organization? Have we worked with them before and if so, what was the impression of those involved? Is there a fee? Who comprises the audience and the other panelists? Is this a topic on which I want to be known, and if not, can the topic be modified?

There are several benefits to speaking engagements that are often overlooked. Not only does the lawyer gain visibility from the talk, but by serving on a panel with colleagues, it provides a chance to demonstrate his or her knowledge to panelists who may be prospective clients or referral sources. In addition, the marketing that supports speaking engagements can often help further promote the lawyer's expertise in the field. Based on the firm's or the lawyer's own philosophy, a mention of the talk can also be placed in a CV or website bio, further highlighting the lawyer's experience. And then when a reporter is looking for an expert on the given topic, and either searches the firm's website or conducts a Google search, the lawyer's name pops up.

Speaking with Reporters

Receiving the unique form of third-party endorsement that comes from appearing as an expert in the press can be very helpful for a lawyer. Like speaking engagements, if appropriately handled, quotes in the media have multiple advantages. It is the type of activity that leads to your name appearing in web searches, and if the quote is substantial, the article may be appropriate to reprint and use for new business purposes. Press also begets press, and a good quote in the right publication can lead to other reporters or conference organizers finding their way to you.

There are myriad nuances to working with the press and it is important for lawyers to receive trained guidance on how to handle these interactions. Reporters can be an influential lot. I've even known of a lawyer hired for a significant engagement due to a reporter's personal recommendation. There is much more about working with the press in the next chapter.

Writing Articles and Whitepapers

Writing longer-form pieces can be useful in building a reputation, though it can take a substantial amount of time. It's essential before jumping into writing something that you, or a PR person with whom you work, check a publication's bylined article guidelines and speak to an editor who oversees the article submission process to determine if this is a topic that interests them. In addition, each publication has its own format and will generally suggest a word count and writing style that works for its readers.

As a marketing person, it's often hard to find a home for a fully baked article. Once a publication choice is located, much like a speaking engagement, the questions to be asked include who is the audience, who else has participated and is there a fee involved?

In addition, it's important to know if the article will be accessible online and if the lawyer or law firm holds the copyright, and if the firm has the right to post the article (with or without a fee) on the firm's website and send it to clients.

Blogs

About five years ago, many lawyers started to launch targeted blogs aimed at getting their ideas and opinions known to a specific community. With the advent of LinkedIn and Twitter, there is a greater opportunity to get blog entries posted in other mediums as well. Blogs can be seen by potential clients as helpful sources of information, but only if they are updated on a regular basis. The law firm Stinson Leonard Street LLP produces a blog called *Arbitration Nation*. It's updated regularly, includes relevant information for those in the field, and is easy to read. It's a great example of a blog fulfilling its mission.

While some clients still view blogs as helpful sources of information, there has been such a proliferation that many have lost the unique standing they once had. While blogs are still a useful source of publishing, as with any law firm publication, they need to strategically find and grow an audience. To do that, the authors must commit to publishing regularly, keeping the blog updated with fresh material and focusing on a carefully defined subject matter. If not, the information will look old and may convey that the firm is out of touch.

Social Media

When handled thoughtfully, social media can be an extremely effective tool, particularly if the lawyer is trying to reach potential influencers or clients in industries such as media, marketing and technology. This topic will be covered in greater detail in the following chapter.

Events

Client events can be terrific, but the "party" part may be the least important aspect. Hosting events that include clients, prospects, referral sources or firm alumni can be very useful if they are planned strategically and there is a specific goal in mind. Lawyers and marketers should focus on the goal of the event by asking themselves at the outset what they want the guests to think about or what it is that they want them to do once they leave the event. What is the ideal outcome?

For example, when holding a dinner for several clients in a private club or room at a restaurant, is the goal to have the clients leave with a stronger impression of the firm's work in the area? Perhaps it's just to get them to be more comfortable with people at the firm with whom they had not previously met. Regardless of what the goal is, a clearly defined goal should inform the structure of the event, who is invited, where is it held, what is discussed and even what type of follow-up will take place after the event.

While events can be difficult to orchestrate, as firm partners struggle over who to invite (e.g., "If I invite Bob, do I have to invite Bob's boss?") and from which partner the invitation should be sent, the struggle is worth it. In professional services marketing, there really is no substitute for the face-to-face interactions that take place. At every well-run client seminar, breakfast briefing, or other such event I have participated in, at least a few pieces of business or connections were garnered. While it may not happen right away, one can usually track business back to these forums.

The quality of the event and having the right people in the room are more critical ingredients than the number of people attending. Prior to an event, lawyers should know who will be attending and key facts about each one's background and their connection to the firm. After an event, it is essential that the lawyers who hosted the event follow up with attendees, by sending personal notes, providing substantive information that may have been promised or scheduling any next-step plans to take advantage of the positive impression that resulted from the event.

Directories

If you are in the legal profession, the names *Legal 500*, *Chambers*, *Lawdragon*, *Benchmark* and *IFLR* are well known. The directories that rank lawyers have become big business, not only for the publishers but also for the law firms that have hired staff to oversee the numerous submissions to these directories. While large law firms may have a half-dozen people who work on submissions, solo practitioners struggle with finding the time to track and complete them. Often the submissions require interviews with practice heads or referral sources (clients who are willing to speak with the directory researchers), and lists of relevant cases, deals, and other matters in which individual partners are involved. It can require a tremendous amount of work to complete the submissions and a great deal of organization to do it in a timely manner. Nevertheless, the hardest part for the marketing department is often not the time-consuming process but the pressure placed on them to get individual lawyers up the ladder on these rankings.

Some law firm lawyers insist that these directories are "a racket" and that they are not used by clients, but I don't believe that is the case. I think the question is not "Do clients use rankings?" but "How do clients use rankings?"

Rieta Ghosh, Managing Editor at Chambers and Partners, remarks, "At Chambers, our goal is to drive excellence in the legal profession globally through our independent research. We work collaboratively with law firm partners and business development teams in making these unbiased assessments and we value the relationships we've formed over the past thirty years. Our research should not be seen as adversarial; we're here to help in-house teams identify those firms that are right for them and can take on that most valued 'trusted advisor' status."

Dan Troy of GlaxoSmithKline confirmed that he does keep copies of the *Legal 500* and *Chambers* in his office. "Reputation still matters a lot," says Dan. "When we look at who we will invite in to our outside counsel initiative, we look at which firms we think are most expert on the matter. Most we know, but we will occasionally look at the directories, just to double check that initial list."

David Burgess reports that the *Legal 500* has the analytics to see who comes online. "I know who the GCs are who are looking at the rankings," he says. It makes sense to David that they are looking. "Think about it in terms of buying a camera. If you are going to buy a new camera, you may first go into a shop to look at the various cameras and talk to the salesperson. Next you look at the web to see reviews and you also look at a camera magazine. Finally, you ring up a friend who is involved in photography and he makes some recommendations. We do this for everything we buy. So, why wouldn't a GC look at the rankings to help make decisions on which law firms or lawyers to use?" he asks, pointing out that when a GC has to select a law firm in a jurisdiction with which she is not familiar, the likelihood she will look at a directory is quite high.

Still, others do not believe the use of directories is a black and white issue. Cahill Gordon's Pierre Gentin, says, "I think in-house lawyers' views of rankings and other professional activities vary widely. When I was a client, I don't recall ever checking whether an outside counsel was ranked by a magazine or directory. On the other hand, substantive and long-term academic, volunteer, professional and creative commitments did mean something to me."

Steve Naifeh is the founder and former CEO of *Best Lawyers*. He points out that while directories are not the only thing a client looks at prior to making a decision, they are a factor. "General counsel are the most sophisticated consumers of legal services and rarely make hiring decisions entirely on the basis of a legal ranking. But *Best Lawyers* and other legal publications help provide third-party validation to general counsel and C-suite clients looking for top legal talent, especially in unfamiliar practice areas or jurisdictions. A credible ranking of a lawyer or a law firm can contribute

LAW FIRM BUSINESS DEVELOPMENT AND MARKETING

important additional information in the hiring process by confirming the lawyer or law firm's standing among their peers," he says.

It seems that every day there are new directories, awards, and submissions cropping up with requests that firms participate in the publication. According to Katrina Dewey, the Founder and CEO of *Lawdragon* and the former Editor of the *LA Daily Journal*, there are several questions that CMOs should ask before agreeing to participate in the rankings of a brand-new publication. Here Katrina asks and answers the questions that firms should consider when a directory comes calling.

1. Is the publication asking you for money to be included? Hard pass.

2. Can you get a higher ranking for more money? Hang up.

3. Who else is being recognized in your category? Only participate in lists with competitors' names whom you genuinely admire and respect.

4. Do they pass the smell test, in other words, are they offering you something too good to be true? We all have egos, and both legitimate rankers and scoundrels play to lawyer ego like fishes to the sea. But there is no single best employment lawyer in the U.S. and the person who claims he was honored as such may have paid $40,000 for it. He is among the very best, but by spending that money, he took himself down many notches among those in the know.

5. Who are these people? Those of us who take your reputation in our hands through awards and distinctions run the gamut from journalists and researchers to marketers and algorithms. Do your research on the methodology and pedigree (if there are any) of those who invite you to participate. While it is true that there are scores of telephone-type directories, there are a handful of respected recognition guides. We offer real research, day-to-day engagement with lawyers and their clients and a full com-

mitment to improving knowledge and choice about legal professionals.

6.   For the bonus points round: How do they handle senior lawyers? Is this an active and vibrant list or a catalog in which you will be featured as part of the Lawyer History archives?

7.   And for the truly savvy, perhaps my most important question — other than the money question: How will your recognition be featured online, and will it be part of your digital reputation in a way of which you will be proud?

In summary, while it is often difficult to measure the return on investment of these tactics, it is possible to monitor metrics such as how many people viewed a particular article, or how many pieces of business resulted from a client event. In addition, firms are able to dig deeper and when a new client has come to the firm, ask how that happened, and what the levers might have been that made it possible. While there will always be difficulty in determining exactly what draws a client to a firm, by employing the right tactics, lawyers certainly have a good running start.

Avoid the Content Trap: Do Less, Accomplish More

By Jamie Diaferia and Andrew Longstreth*

There are any number of ways for law firms to get the attention of the media, clients and prospects, but one of the most reliable is to produce original, engaging content.

In theory, this sounds easy. And in one sense, it *is* easy. Never before have there been so many cheap tools to create content. Newsletters, blogs, white papers, client alerts, webinars, podcasts, videos — they're all available options to law firms these days.

But it's one thing to produce original content, and quite another to produce content that matters to the wider world. That's why we advise law firms to carefully choose editorial projects that can have lasting value beyond a news cycle. In other words, we tell them to say no to lots of shallow projects and yes to a few ambitious ones.

Our thinking on the subject has been influenced by a book called *Deep Work: Rules for Focused Success in a Distracted World* by Cal Newport. As media junkies who often feel helpless to resist the siren calls of Twitter and breaking news alerts, we found its insights and recommendations for cultivating sustained focus valuable.

But it's the book's underlying premise that most interested us: Work of lasting value — the kind that our society (clients, too) values and rewards the most — requires a sustained commitment to deep work.

This is intuitive, of course. We instinctively understand that when, for example, Ron Chernow was writing his best-selling

---

* Jamie Diaferia, the CEO and founder of Infinite Global, helps professional services firms and their clients with high-stakes communications matters. Andrew Longstreth is Head Writer for Infinite Global where he creates custom content for professional services firms.

biography on Alexander Hamilton or his latest on Ulysses S. Grant, he wasn't simultaneously trying to maintain an active presence on social media.

But here's a slightly subtler point by Newport: In our digital age — in which we have so many distractions competing for our attention — this skill of extended focus has atrophied in many of us, imperiling our ability to achieve the kind of success we want.

Here's how Newport defines deep work: "Professional activities performed in a state of distraction-free concentration that push your cognitive capacities to their limit. These efforts create new value, improve your skill, and are hard to replicate."

As law firm marketers, this concept applies to us, too. Ultimately, the biggest rewards in our industry will not be reserved for those who can perform a lot of inch-deep tasks. They will be reserved for those who can conceive and execute grand projects that delight and provide value that can't be found elsewhere. In other words, only those with a deep work ethos will accomplish projects that people remember.

Law firm content producers should heed this warning. But as content becomes more central to their marketing goals, law firms should not interpret that mandate to mean simply producing more content, especially the kind that can already easily be found in the marketplace — the kind that does not require much deep work. That choice may allow firms to feel like they've checked a box, but it likely won't produce lasting value.

The reality is that producing high-quality content that breaks through to the media, prospects and clients is getting harder as the volume and level of competition increases.

The *Economist* recently polled more than 1,600 marketers and senior executives worldwide about the state of thought leadership, and the results reflected this intense competition. It found that 75% of executives have become more selective about the thought leadership they consume, with more than 80% citing the increase in volume as the reason.

When advising law firms, we like to talk about the signal-to-noise ratio. To stand out, some firms may need to decrease the volume of content they produce to devote more resources to projects that require deep work but will cut through the noise.

In his book, Newport references work from the authors of *The 4 Disciplines of Execution*, who have noted, "the more you try to do, the less you actually accomplish."[1] That's why, they suggest, organizations are better served when they focus on a few wildly ambitious goals.

A law firm content strategy should largely reflect the strategy of the firm itself. For many firms, executing that strategy likely will mean producing content that fits the goals of key practice areas. But a strategy should also contemplate a signature project — a wildly ambitious goal requiring deep work — that best reflects the firm's brand, stakes out territory it wants to own, and provides the media, clients and prospective clients with real and lasting value.

It's important to note what this type of content should not be. It should not be marketing puffery celebrating the firm's accomplishments or mere summaries of legal proceedings or industry trends.

These kinds of ambitious projects must be laser-focused on providing singular insights that cannot be found elsewhere. This is a high bar to clear, for sure, but that's the point.

While not an exhaustive list, here are a few elements to think about including in such a project:

Original data and analysis: This element can take a number of different forms: a survey, an index, original packaging of publicly available data, etc. The key is that the data be presented in a unique format and that the data is accompanied with interpretation that tells the reader what it all means. Original research is of inherent interest to the press, whose coverage can greatly increase the reach of the project.

1.　CHRIS McCHESNEY, SEAN COVEY & JIM HULING, THE 4 DISCIPLINES OF EXECUTION (Free Press 2012), at 10.

Outside perspectives: These projects should be used as opportunities to highlight a firm's experts. But there is no reason not to also include perspectives from people with no ties to the firm. Again, the primary focus should be on providing real value to the customer first, not promoting the firm.

Rich media mixed with snackable content: Ambitious editorial projects need to contemplate a mix of available media. Today, an interview need not be just a written Q&A; it can also be a podcast or a video. Similarly, thought leadership is not simply a print product. Quotes, sound bites, data points, and other snackable content taken from the anchor piece can be repurposed through social media channels.

Chapter 8

Traditional and Social Media

In the late 1980s, the Jurassic days of legal media, there were three big players based in New York City. At the *New York Times*, the sharp-witted David Margolick was writing his weekly "At the Bar" column, demystifying the operations of the legal profession. Downtown at the *Wall Street Journal*, Deputy Managing Editor Steven Adler was overseeing much of the paper's legal coverage. And at the *American Lawyer*, the innovator Steven Brill held the reins. On the West Coast, activity was starting to brew. Charles Munger, who owned the *LA Daily Journal*, was about to launch *California Law Business*.

The Media Is the Message: Different Types of Press

Today, there are dozens of publications covering the legal profession, and even more reporting on narrow legal topics, such as court decisions, arbitrations, corporate transactions, and other related news. *Above the Law*, a legal website launched by David Lat in 2006, provides up-to-the-minute behind-the-scenes news in the world of Big Law. *Law360* publishes numerous daily newsletters and legal news, reporting from multiple bureaus across the country. Several other news publications fall under the American Lawyer

Media (ALM) umbrella, including *Legal Week*, *Corporate Counsel* and the *National Law Journal*. Add to that an additional layer enabled by technology, including other websites, blogs, Twitter groups, and listservs from which lawyers get their news, and there is today a robust market of legal coverage.

The media landscape is continuously changing. Bill Carter of ALM says, "We've recently changed our operation to be more responsive to the market, and a bit more like a B-to-B company. We have several media properties, so we face the challenge of looking for greater efficiencies. We asked ourselves, could we have beat reporters who work in a global newsroom, so that even with the success of these great publications, these talented people can work and scale their insights together? By doing that, we can focus on more topics and report more effectively. Today's news pieces need to be short and impactful. They must be packed with data."

For a marketer or lawyer who wants to see her story in the press, there are choices as to where to head to publicize a story. The same is true for those who embark down the advertising path. There are lots and lots of options.

Traditionally, there were three classes of media: geographic; industry or trade; and business. Today, those categories are much more fluid due to the advent of technology and the ability for publishers of all types to segment markets into ever smaller bites.

According to the Pew Research Center, about four in ten Americans get their news regularly online.[1] Due to the reach of the web, traditional general newspapers, like the *New York Times* and the *Dallas Morning News*, are available around the globe and online, so they are no longer truly geographically focused. Industry publications still exist, such as *Automotive News* for the auto industry, *Pharmacy Times* for the pharmaceutical industry and the *American Lawyer* for the legal profession. Business press used to refer to *Reuters*, *Fortune* and the *Wall Street Journal*, but with beat report-

---

1.   Modern News Consumer, survey conducted January 12–February 8, 2016.

ers and special pull-out sections, they no longer merely cover the business of being in business. In any given day's edition of the *Wall Street Journal,* you are just as likely to see an article about restaurants in Hong Kong as you are about the Federal Reserve Bank's interest rate increase. And in the legal press, publications such as the *New York Law Journal* or *Legal Business* in London may cover a specific region or the entire globe.

Most often when public relations professionals — whether in-house at a law firm or at an outside agency — handle a story about a lawyer or law firm, they'll consider several approaches before they begin to contact reporters at the various publications that may have an interest. They will often think of the story in terms of its relevance to the different classes of geographic, industry and business press. For example, if the lawyer is involved in a significant litigation issue affecting the automotive industry, *Automotive News* and the *American Lawyer* may both be possible industry publications to target, but if the case involves a car plant in Michigan, they may also want to reach out to a regional press outlet, like the *Detroit Free Press.*

Jamie Diaferia of Infinite Global, states, "If a lawyer, for example, wants to get referrals from other lawyers, the legal press may make more sense. For attorneys interested in becoming known in certain industries, the business press may make more sense. There is often overlap in what interests the business and legal press, so it's not typically wise to ignore one over the other."

There is also a growing school of thought that in the end, where the story first appears may not make too much of a difference. Once the content appears online, a piece can be shared via email, Twitter, and LinkedIn. The author can target the audience he or she wants simply by sharing and reposting.

On the other end of the press spectrum — because the web has enabled even more people to publish — there is a growth of micro-publishers, those who are writing and publishing for a small and specialized audience. With blogs and online publications, there is an ability to cover small subsections of industry and geography as never before. In addition, there are more opportunities for lawyers to make a name for themselves by creating their own targeted communication with influencers and potential clients. So, while this means marketers have more places in which to get one of their lawyers mentioned, it also suggests that there is an opportunity to self-publish and create narrow bands of self-publications. One such example is *Dashboard Insights*, a targeted and well-defined auto industry law blog produced by Foley & Lardner LLP.

Regardless of the media outlet that covers a story, how an audience — whether it be a general counsel or a law firm recruit — receives the information has changed as well. It's easy for consumers of media to customize their newsfeeds, set up Google alerts, and read press highlights just by following Twitter. We each have the chance to curate what we want to read and how we want to read it.

Getting Quoted

How is it that time after time, it seems like a handful of the same lawyers are quoted in the press? There is an easy explanation: relationships. A reporter may first call a lawyer as a source on a story because the reporter has heard the lawyer's name through the grapevine, read an article that she bylined, or received her phone number from a PR person. Reporters want to call experts they respect and who are likely to provide insight for a story. Just as important though, they need sources who will respond promptly. Chances are the reporter is under a deadline. If they have a relationship with a source, and the source has a reputation of quickly returning phone calls, they are likely to call that source on a regular basis.

In today's 24/7 world, reporters compete against one another to be the first ones out of the gate to break a story. It's often the case that in the midst of working on a story, a reporter will place calls to several sources to get their input. Whichever source first returns the call may be more likely to be the one to be quoted. These lawyers know that when a reporter calls, they need to respond quickly.

Often the lawyers we see quoted are those who have established long-term relationships with reporters. Like the relationship between a client and their lawyer, a relationship with a reporter needs to be a reciprocal one, fostered over time.

We've all heard lawyers say that there are conflicts with clients that preclude them from speaking with the media. Most in-house PR people have a system set up with their records department or key partners (or both) so that they can ensure that the firm is not talking about an existing or potential client. Potential conflicts get particularly sticky with litigation because even if there isn't a direct client conflict, a lawyer would never want to publicly espouse a position that runs counter to one she might take with a current or future client. At a minimum, lawyers need to be very sensitive to these issues.

There may be times when a lawyer can't publicly comment for a particular story. Perhaps there is a real or implied client conflict on an issue, or one of the parties covered in the story has some relationship to the firm. I always err on the side of caution with these decisions. In these situations, the lawyer may still want to talk to the reporter, but may only be able to do so off the record, or on the record but without attribution. Or the lawyer might offer to talk not about the specifics of the matter but in a more academic way, describing the impact of a decision or the stages of civil procedure. The reporter may welcome the chance to hear a lawyer's insight on an issue, or an explanation of the implication of relevant facts. There are many options when working with reporters. Regardless of what will be discussed, these terms should be agreed upon at the *start* of the interview.

Off the record can mean many different things. It may mean that the reporter will simply use the information provided by the interview subject, but without attribution. In other cases, a reporter may agree to an off-the-record interview if the interview subject in turn agrees that the reporter can use the subject's comments if he or she runs them by the subject after the interview.

Thus, "off the record" can have different meanings to reporters, as well as to lawyers and to PR folks, and that is why any discussion with a reporter should begin by carefully defining what each side expects. Again, these are subtle yet important distinctions and should be covered at the start of any interview as part of a discussion of ground rules with a reporter.

Social Media: The Frontier

To date, I am not a big fan of lawyers using Facebook for business purposes, but I do think there is a good case to be made for using LinkedIn and, for certain areas of practice, Twitter and Instagram. While some firms are slow to adapt to social media, others are using it to great advantage. They are building robust alumni groups on LinkedIn, and getting their firm's news out on multiple channels, including Twitter and Instagram.

"Ultimately, the goal of social media activity should be to drive engagement with a firm's clients, not just add to the noise. Law firms don't need to be on every social media site — just the ones that are relevant to their clients."

—Jamie Diaferia, Infinite Global

Posting a profile on LinkedIn is an excellent way for potential clients to see a lawyer's professional background. Some lawyers still have a hard time accepting that LinkedIn is important for profile-building. But several recent statistics demonstrate why the platform matters so much. According to BTI, 76.6% of GCs and CLOs use LinkedIn. A 2018 Greentarget Zeughauser study reported that 42% of GCs say LinkedIn profiles are somewhat important when researching lawyers and law firms for potential hires.[2] And a 2017 Attorney at Work Survey reported that 84% of lawyers who responded maintained a profile on LinkedIn.[3] With those statistics in mind, from both a competitive and practical standpoint, it makes sense for lawyers to have an accurate, complete, and up-to-date profile.

LinkedIn has become a good way for lawyers to stay connected with a wide range of contacts. With the appropriate safeguards put into place, it can be an effective way of keeping in touch with people with whom you hope to develop or expand business. But the safeguards are important. For example, lawyers should set up their account to ensure that others can't see their connections. This is important if you've connected on LinkedIn with clients. It's obviously best to keep those names private.

Used judiciously, LinkedIn can also be a great tool for reminding people of a lawyer's expertise. Linking to or posting articles, or commenting on articles or comments by others can help the lawyer keep top of mind with contacts while reinforcing his or her position in the marketplace.

Jeff Klein at Weil Gotshal regularly posts pieces about his area of practice. Jeff says, "Business-oriented social media can give readers insights that help them differentiate between lawyers and firms, provide them with a broader perspective as to who you are as a lawyer and a person, and demonstrate the substantive areas in which you have expertise and on which you focus." But Jeff warns, "If you're too broad in your social media posting, you are a jack of all trades, master of none, and if you use social media imprudently or

---

2.   2018 State of Digital & Content Marketing Survey, http://greentarget.com/stateofdigital/#about.

3.   Social Media Marketing Survey Report, https://www.attorneyatwork.com/wp-content/uploads/2017/03/2017-Social-Media-Marketing-Survey-Report-@-AttorneyatWork.pdf.

without discipline, you can tarnish your reputation and lower your followers' expectations of the quality of your advice."

While traditional PR will not go away, it can be supplemented and enhanced by the use of social media. Social media is one way of furthering a lawyer or firm's brand through the approach called "thought leadership." The term refers to focusing on just a few key areas in which a lawyer excels, and demonstrating his or her expertise on a regular basis through writing and speaking in those areas.

Guy Alvarez, Founder and CEO of Good2bSocial, LLC says, "You can't name yourself a thought leader. *Other* people need to call you a thought leader. I've talked to various accomplished leaders who will say, 'I am the expert in X.' I then ask them what type of content they have been publishing. If they are not, well, they need to begin to participate within their circles of influence. It used to be that lawyers hired PR people to get them online, but with technology today, you no longer need to rely on intermediaries. You can build your own thought leadership platform. It's a much more direct route."

Lee Garfinkle of Allen & Overy is a big advocate for the use of technology and keeps an astute eye on law firms' use of digital media. He believes that firms are all across the board regarding their digital marketing and social media adoption. "For social media, I see firms falling into one of four categories: Level one firms don't use social media at all, and that's a missed opportunity for them. Level two firms are those that flirt with social media and typically have a small presence with static content, but they don't update content regularly. Level three firms use social media as a communications distribution channel and push firm content the way they likely do with traditional media and their website. The most digitally advanced firms — the level four firms — are engaged, participatory, and are active community members on the platforms that work best for them. For these firms, social media is not just a channel to push content, but rather, a place to have a dialogue with their clients, prospects, recruits and alumni. Few firms are at level four," he says.

Jamie Diaferia says, "Social media can be viewed as an amplification tool. Traditionally, law firms had limited ways to distribute their content. With social media, firms can extract more value from their content by exposing it to more people. Ultimately, the goal of social media activity should be to drive engagement with a firm's clients, not just add to the noise. Law firms don't need to be on every social media site — just the ones that are relevant to their clients."

Twitter can be a good way to make a name for oneself in a specific niche. Bob Ambrogi is a media and technology lawyer. Every few hours he seems to be tweeting. He has 18,000 followers and is followed by a wide span of legal media.

Firms are also using Twitter in unique ways. The law firm Allens, which has offices in Australia and Asia, tweets every couple of hours.

Skadden pays close attention on Twitter to reflect its strong graphic identity, and it has a thoughtful Twitter feed aimed solely at law school students. It's unclear why other firms do not do this when they know that they are recruiting a generation of people who get their information from social media.

Kristin Calve is the co-founder of Law Business Media. "With Twitter, it is essential to develop and maintain an authentic voice within the community. Don't just post and retweet without adding valuable commentary or context. When sharing thought leadership, it is ideal to post content multiple times in order to have the highest impact. Leverage key industry events by live-tweeting, riding their hashtags with relevant content, and engaging with others in the Twitter-sphere," she says.

Lawyers can use social media both as a tool to communicate and as a way to listen to their constituents and monitor feedback. By monitoring Twitter, LinkedIn, and other social media, lawyers can get an idea of what is being said about the firm in the public domain.

And during a time of a firm crisis, social media is even more important. It becomes essential to monitor what is happening in real time to be aware of both who is communicating about the situation and the substance of what they are saying. There are many social media tools for monitoring this activity, and a good PR agency can provide guidance on how best to do this. But if a firm in the midst of a crisis does not watch social media carefully, it can sink the firm quite quickly.

Between Google Analytics and Twitter Analytics, there is a lot of information out there that allows users to measure the impact of their social media campaigns. Steve Spiess at Brownstein Hyatt says, "We now publish quarterly a series of graphics on those analytics, showing all of the web hits for people in the firm. We can tell how they are doing in the various departments and practice areas. It creates an eye-opening experience and people see for themselves that it is important to have a web presence these days."

While face-to-face communication is still the gold standard of keeping in touch with contacts (and the lost art of letter writing may be the silver), social media allows lawyers to connect with important contacts and prospects. It is an effective way to strategically grow networks as it provides an opportunity to share and let people know what you want them to know in a nonintrusive way.

Stefanie Marrone, Director of Business Development and Marketing at Tarter Krinsky & Drogin LLP and an experienced social media advisor, reminds firms to show versus tell. "Every piece of content you post should be value-added, helpful and client-centric. Don't just tell your clients why you are the very best lawyers, *show them*." She believes that all writing, particularly for social media, should be done with this in mind. "Remember that many times, your clients are not lawyers. Always put yourself in their shoes. Throw the legalese out the window. Clients want to know who you are and how you can help them. Think about *how to demonstrate* that you are a leader in your field versus telling someone."

Think Piece

Using Twitter to Learn, Build a Name, and Grow Relationships

By Kevin O'Keefe*

Twitter, with 330 million users, is the people's news and information network.

For lawyers, Twitter represents a golden opportunity — to learn, build a name, and grow relationships.

From Twitter's co-founder Jack Dorsey:

"Twitter is what's happening, and what everyone is talking about (literally!). News and talk. We're the people's news network. People choose us for news because we're the fastest. Fastest to get news, and fastest to share news with the whole world."[1]

Twitter is also becoming the first place people, including lawyers, check for news and information. In many cases, Twitter is the only source for information, via "citizen journalists" with a smartphone in remote places of the world, on a street corner or in a courtroom.

---

*   Trial lawyer turned legal tech entrepreneur, Kevin O'Keefe is Founder and CEO of Seattle-based, LexBlog, Inc., which is building the world's largest and most comprehensive legal news and information network by drawing on the contributions of legal bloggers worldwide.

1.   Internal memo of Jack Dorsey. *See* Sarah Frier & Mark Gurman, *Twitter's Dorsey Rallies Staff Around Independent Strategy in Internal Memo*, BLOOMBERG (Oct. 10, 2016), https://www.bloomberg.com/news/articles/2016-10-10/twitter-s-dorsey-rallies-staff-around-independent-strategy-in-internal-memo.

Learn

Twitter is a more professional news network than Facebook and a better place than LinkedIn for professionals to follow information.

A tweet of the maximum 280 characters is often more than sufficient for sharing and reading information and commentary.

Dennis Garcia, Assistant General Counsel at Microsoft, says Twitter represents a "growth mindset" for lawyers and provides them a wonderful opportunity to gain knowledge and learn.

It has become my primary news feed as I follow over 700 Twitter accounts that provide me with the latest information I need about my company, our customers/competitors/partners and the legal environment in general so that I can provide more impactful legal advice to my business clients.[2]

Beyond the news and information, itself, Twitter enables lawyers to select sources of news and information they trust — colleagues, friends, bloggers, mainstream reporters, company leaders, scientists, doctors, academics and publishers.

Twitter, used effectively, funnels the volume of online information. By finding "intelligence agents" who sift through online news and information and share relevant items on Twitter, lawyers get a custom AP news feed on their niche.

You find such "intelligence agents" by searching on Google for influential Twitter users on niches and looking at who those Twitter users follow and cite on Twitter.

Follow a manageable number of people for your Twitter feed to be of value. Though you may only look at your main Twitter feed occasionally (once or twice a day, every couple days), following thousands of users will render your feed a fire hose.

---

2. Dennis Garcia, *What Lawyers Can Learn From the SCOTUS Nominee Twitter Campaign*, https://www.lexblog.com/2016/03/24/what-lawyers-can-learn-from-the-scotus-nominee-twitter-campaign/.

Twitter is not a social network where protocol dictates that you follow everyone who follows you. When deciding to follow someone, ask yourself if what they are sharing would be of value.

In many cases, your best sources for filtering news and information will have far more people following them on Twitter than they'll be following in return.

Build a Name

Twitter for building a name means identifying a niche passion. What area of the law or business would you like to be known for? Locally, statewide, nationally or worldwide.

By sharing on Twitter what you are reading and seeing on your niche, Twitter users will see value in what you are sharing. You will build your own professional brand and develop a network of followers.

You'll be further discovered as Twitter's algorithms highlight for other Twitter users relevant news (including items you share) and sources (you as a regular sharer on a niche).

You become "the source" or at least one of the sources, by focusing on a tight niche. Think international IP issues arising from animated video characters. Medical malpractice/product liability for a particular heart valve. Teenage custody in family law.

Finding and staying abreast of niche news and information to share on Twitter is easy. Follow sources (blogs and traditional media) and subjects (keywords and phrases) on Feedly, a news aggregator.

Alternatively, use Twitter to feed you news by using Twitter searches, creating Twitter lists of users who share on relevant niches, or following a small number of Twitter users, in general.

Grow Relationships

Despite common belief that social media is all about mindshare, attention and broadcasting to get attention or web traffic, social media is about relationships.

Look at content, whether a share on Twitter or a blog post, as the currency for relationships, as opposed to the end goal.

Twitter is an outstanding network for building relationships. Relationships for professional growth. Relationships for business development. And relationships for learning.

Because of the limited effort in "publishing" on Twitter, versus a blog post or article, you have more people "publishing" and the opportunity to get to know more people.

Nowhere will you develop relationships with more interesting and diverse people from around the world than on Twitter. Whether across town or across the ocean, you will get to know people online and face to face who will inspire you and help you become a better lawyer.

Don't just take my word for it. From Garcia:

"Twitter can help grow your professional network. Since I've been using Twitter I've met many people that I probably would not have met via other forms of social media or on my own."[3]

Be strategic in building relationships on Twitter. Follow on Feedly the names of people and companies with whom you want to develop relationships. Share on Twitter, with your take, what they are saying or the news you are reading about them. Include their Twitter handle so they see you talking about them via an email and notification from Twitter. They'll respond with a virtual handshake.

Follow keywords and phrases (subjects) on Feedly and share on Twitter who is writing what about whom and about what. Share on Twitter the relevant items with your commentary. Again include

---

3. *Id.*

the Twitter handle for these people, companies, associations, and sources. You'll get responses.

Follow on Twitter the people and organizations with whom you'd like to develop a relationship. Retweet what they are saying, including your point of view.

Look at Twitter as a conversation. Maybe better, a room, where unlike at a networking event, you feel at ease. People have common interests, people know each other, and people trust each other.

Twitter is a great place for lawyers to learn, build a name, and grow relationships.

Chapter 9

Women and Marketing

Breaking the Glass Ceiling of Business Development

Despite the fact that women and men have been enrolled in law school in relatively equal numbers for several years — and in 2016, for the first time, there were more women than men enrolled[1] — such parity does not yet exist in the top roles in the profession, whether at law firms or as general counsel at corporations. According to a 2017 study by the National Association of Women Lawyers (NAWL), despite being hired at the associate level in nearly equal numbers as men, women are still the minority of both equity (19%) and non-equity (30%) law firm partners. When they become partner, the story for women doesn't improve. Women still comprise only 25% of law firm governance roles and only 25% of general counsel positions. While commitment to gender diversity is at an all-time high, statistics show that there is still much progress to be made.

However, there is hope for the profession. The ABA, Minority Corporate Counsel Association (MCCA), local bar associations, and many other related organizations around the world are study-

---

1. Elizabeth Olson, *Women Make Up Majority of U.S. Law Students for the First Time*, N.Y. Times (Dec. 16, 2016).

ing this issue. They are making recommendations and pushing for change. In 2016, NAWL issued the One-Third by 2020 Challenge, renewing the call for the legal profession to increase its representation of women to at least one-third among Fortune 1000 general counsel, new law firm equity partners, law firm lateral hires, and law school deans. Clients are starting to demand that the firms they hire demonstrate diverse teams. The media is requesting that firms give transparency to their diversity statistics. Law firms are making efforts, and those efforts are slowly making a difference.

Firms with established women's initiatives seem to have a higher percentage of women equity partners than those just launching these types of initiatives. There is good reason. Some firms have been at this for a while, and that is encouraging. Skadden Arps is one such firm. Just one element of its initiative that has received high praise involves bringing its women partners and clients together for an annual retreat involving thought-provoking speakers and the sharing of education and ideas.

But on a profession-wide basis, more needs to happen for the situation to change, and viable solutions need to be brought to the table. Judge Shira Scheindlin made news with a 2017 *New York Times* Op-Ed piece in which she described those who litigated cases before her in court. She wrote, "In the 22 years I spent on the federal bench before stepping down last year, not much changed when it came to listening to lawyers. The talking was almost always done by white men. Women often sat at counsel table but were usually junior and silent. It was a rare day when a woman had a lead role — even though women have made up about half of law school graduates since the early 1990s."[2]

Business development may hold one of the keys to helping with the issue of advancement of women. Developing a practice with a

---

2. Shira Scheindlin, *Female Lawyers Can Talk, Too*, N.Y. Times (Aug. 8, 2017), https://www.nytimes.com/2017/08/08/opinion/female-lawyers-women-judges.html.

solid book of business increases one's power within an organization. Slowly, we are seeing women lawyers with strong client relationship and rainmaking abilities become leaders in firms; others are being plucked liked gems as pricey lateral partners. While more work needs to be done in this area, business development and the ability to market can help jumpstart a career.

Networking

The concept of networking taking place at the golf course is not dead, as many believe that the concept of men networking with other men continues, just often off the course. "Let's go to a hockey game," or "Can we grab a beer?" are still familiar refrains between men and their clients. Sometimes women are included in those invitations, but more often they are not.

There is an adage that people gravitate to and like to work with people who are the most familiar to them, or most like them. Unfortunately, when men network solely with other men, and women only with other women, both sides miss out on the networking that can be done with more diverse groups. The most significant negative impact of gender-specific networking is felt by women. If men still control the majority of a law firm's business relationships, and most GCs are male, a young man networking with an older man will have greater access to clients, while the younger woman networking with an older woman will have less access.

Networking and the development of alliances are critical in developing business. Qualitative experience tells us that lawyers with a greater ability to get to know other people and make investments in relationships are much more likely to become rainmakers. But networking in the form of inviting people out for breakfast or lunch and asking for a piece of business can be an uncomfortable activity for someone who is not used to doing it. There is a general impression from consultants and coaches that women are more concerned than men that if they stick their heads out or cause too much attention to be paid to themselves, it will backfire.

There can be enormous value in women's networking events, and it is important to have women work together to learn from and empower one another to succeed. But women-only programs without other types of support are limited in what they can accomplish. It is important for women lawyers to have access to partners who are effective business developers. Networking, mentorship and sponsorship should continue beyond the women's event, and cross over the gender divide.

Mentorship Versus Sponsorship

There is a big difference between mentorship and sponsorship. Mentorship is when a professional provides advice, guidance, and feedback by taking someone deserving under their wing. Sponsorship is when the deserving person is helped, introduced, and supported in their goals. They are given opportunities, not merely encouragement. Ida Abbott is a former litigation partner turned consultant in the professional services arena and the author of *Sponsoring Women: What Men Need to Know*.[3] She is also co-founder of the Hastings Leadership Academy for Women at the University of California Hastings College of Law. Ida notes, "While firms have been active in creating mentorship programs where they connect a junior and senior partner, sponsorship has typically happened on a more organic basis. There is a big difference between the impact of the two types of relationships." She explains, "Sponsorship is a much more assertive and interventional activity. If I am mentoring you, I would say 'It is important for you go get to know Charlie. Chances are he can send you some work.' Then you walk out to figure it out for yourself. If I am sponsoring you, I

---

3.   Ida O. Abbott and Attorney at Work (2014).

would say, 'You need to get to know Charlie. I'm having lunch with him and want to bring you along to talk about your ideas.'"

In short, a mentor can give good advice, but a sponsor can be an advocate. It's especially helpful for women lawyers to seek out others who are willing to serve as their sponsor.

Diversity Within the Firm

It's important for lawyers to be cognizant of putting together diverse work teams and pitch groups within a firm. The purpose is not only for inclusion but to produce teams that will cultivate better ideas and provide more creative problem-solving. In an ideal world, partners would create diverse teams on their own, and firms would send reminders and guidelines to encourage partners to do so. Ida believes that even with these "nudges," firms should have mechanisms in place to review proposed teams for diversity. This can be done through the marketing department, a professional development function or within practice groups.

Marketing Training

Most lawyers, male or female, can benefit from marketing help. While lawyers may prefer focusing on doing the work, often they wait to address marketing when they learn there is a dire necessity to develop business. By then, they may be stuck in a routine, and playing catch-up becomes even more difficult as it is also generally accompanied by a change in marketplace that forces them to develop this new skill. Marketing training becomes a particularly valuable tool for women and should be provided early on in their careers before limiting behaviors are set in stone.

The ABA has done much in advancing women in the profession through its Commission on Women in the Profession. The mission of the ABA Commission is to secure the full and equal participation of women in the legal profession and the justice system, so that there is a robust array of women in all sectors and all levels including the most senior positions. The Commission provides many different types of support. Part of that is developing the programs and tools for educating legal employers about best practices to retain and advance women, and women lawyers about pathways to success.

Stephanie Scharf, who leads the law firm Scharf Banks Marmor LLC and is chair of the ABA Commission, says, "Many women lawyers would benefit by having help, in strategizing, planning, and implementing business development activities." At her firm, a marketing consultant is made available to every lawyer. Stephanie feels strongly that since many lawyers think they are not naturally skilled at marketing, or for one reason or another do not like to market, they need additional support to help them reach outside their comfort zones. The firm provides this option and most men and women have used it, advancing their own careers and of course helping to grow the firm.

Much of what training can do is to help women to say "no" to those activities that will not make sense for them. Consultant Silvia Coulter of LawVision Group says, "Women constantly get asked to be on committees or are asked to be involved in other non-billable activities. Teaching someone to ask to be taken off a committee is vital. It is so freeing." Silvia points out that women want to be viewed as team players and they don't relish the idea of being assertive and turning something down.

Training by consultants involves a lot of interaction through role-playing and exercises. Often partners are interviewed in advance to help set the stage. A byproduct of the training, especially when done in co-ed groups, is that it can uncover and address inherent biases. Training should focus on what makes lawyers authentically comfortable in a sales role. It's important to examine that thinking in order to be better able to play better in the sandbox.

Traits: Advantages or Challenges?

Stephanie says, "Too often, women experience impediments. Some are internal and involve how they feel about marketing, and some are simply due to a lack of training about what to do and what to say in a selling scenario. Other impediments are structural. Many women are cut out of marketing opportunities, or their time is used to front other firm initiatives, so they don't get the experience and rewards that come with regular marketing activities."

"Women tend to keep their heads down and say, 'I am going to do impressive work.' But networking both externally and internally is very important. Just going to lunch or creating ways of connecting with their colleagues and partners is a good idea. It keeps you in the loop on all types of developments."

—Stephanie Scharf, Scharf Banks Marmor LLC, and ABA Commission on Women in the Profession

---

Stephanie points out that most lawyers — men and women — are fearful when they first need to sell themselves or their firms. "The reality is," says Stephanie, "that some lawyers are doing marketing every single day, although it is not typically women who are doing so." Stephanie recalls, "I once phoned a general counsel whom I had been calling every few months just to check in and see how things were going for him. I hadn't yet worked with his company, but I wanted to find a way. I felt awkward and actually apologized to him at one point simply for making the call. He stopped the conversation and said, 'Look, the guys are calling me every two weeks and you should be, too.' I learned from that and now I don't apologize anymore. I finally came to understand, it's my business to follow up. It's like in the movie *The Godfather*, 'It's just business.' People need to make their peace with marketing."

While it may be a generalization, Stephanie points out that on the impediment side, women tend to overprepare for marketing efforts and often fail to prioritize the importance of networking the way men often do. Stephanie says, "Women tend to keep their heads down and say, 'I am going to do impressive work.' But networking both externally and internally is very important. Just going to lunch or creating ways of connecting with their colleagues and partners is a good idea. It keeps you in the loop on all types of developments."

Stephanie encourages everyone at her firm, men and women, to be involved in organizations, volunteer for roles in various groups, and author articles. She knows that by doing so they will develop a substantive reputation which will help them market, and that by taking roles in organizations, they will meet new people and develop a host of other skills.

Women can be very good at establishing and fostering relationships, and those relationship-building characteristics can also help with likability. Bonnie Ciaramella, management consultant and CEO of Ciaramella & Co. LLC, points out, "When you are choosing a lawyer, obviously he or she has to have the skills, but the likability factor and relationship-building ability are key. Women generally have a great ability to listen and pay attention to details. Those skills are essential and advantageous in developing relationships."

Silvia Coulter got her start in consulting as a salesperson and knows in her DNA what makes a good salesperson. Silvia says that the necessary skill set is the same for men and women, but "the key is to really work with people to understand their style and personality. Women are often great nurturers, and by tapping into that, they have done very well in sales within a lot of industries because of these traits."

Catherine McGregor, Editor-in-Chief of the MCCA publication, *Diversity & the Bar* says, "There are many routes to developing
business and it's about finding the one that works best for you.
For example, many women feel quite uncomfortable with the traditional notion of 'working a room' but might prefer to network on
a more one-to-one basis."

Clients Demanding Change

As is the case with other changes in the legal profession, clients
may be the ones who force firms to change regarding the role of
women, both in firm leadership and in client matters. Clients recognize that building diverse groups is not simply a matter of corporate responsibility or optics, but one of creating intelligent teams.

Those inside of corporations have read the same studies that
their law firm counterparts have read. Both sides know that diverse
teams have the power to lead companies to better performance,
return on investment, and overall profitability. Teams composed of
individuals with different backgrounds are more likely to reexamine
facts in new and intelligent ways.

Publications that are read by clients, such as the *American
Lawyer* and the rankings publication the *Legal 500*, are asking law
firms to report diversity information. David Burgess, editor of the
Legal 500 says, "Diversity information will give clients the opportunity they need to make educated decisions when selecting a law
firm. We want to provide information on gender, ethnicity, LGBT,
and disability. We want to look at it across the partner and associate
populations and also try to incorporate the firms' success rates with
these groups. We want to know if these groups are being hired by
law firms and how long on average will they stay there."

Dan Troy of GlaxoSmithKline says that his team is wary of
the bait-and-switch game that law firms can play when bringing a
diverse group of people to a pitch. Ensuring that outside counsel
truly uses a diverse team is so important that Dan and his team
track the individuals who are presented to them at the pitch, and

if the firm is hired, how those individuals were actually involved in the matter. Over time, he can see how the firms are doing on a number of matters. Dan says, "We look at diversity on both the front end and the back end of the assignment."

Authenticity in Marketing

Firms need to go beyond placing words on their website. Catherine Alman MacDonagh says, "If you are going to promote that you have a women's initiative or have a commitment to diversity, you need to do more than just articulate those values. You must do an exceptional job at actually engaging in the behaviors that demonstrate the commitment." She points out that in-house counsel care about the data and they want accurate statistics. "They will go beyond reading flowery language," says Catherine. "They want to know how many women leaders there are and in what roles. We need to be sure we are doing the right things in the first place, then put those metrics in place, and become more capable at reporting the numbers and actual examples."

For many years, Debevoise has led the profession in promoting women's professional development and leadership at the firm. Just a look at its current letterhead shows that it is not just giving this lip service: Senior Chair (Mary Jo White), Co-Chair, Litigation Department (Mary Beth Hogan), Deputy Chair, Corporate Department (Nicole Levin Mesard), Co-Head, Private Equity Group (Rebecca F. Silberstein), Chair, Restructuring Practice (M. Natasha Labovitz), and the list goes on. While Debevoise does a lot to promote the fact that it cares about retaining and developing its women — by creating micro-websites, events, and newsletters dedicated to women — its words are substantive and based on fact. As one of the first large firms to make a part-time lawyer a partner, and the home of the first woman president of the City Bar, the firm can responsibly hold out examples of institutional and individual success.

Pryor Cashman LLP is another firm that does an outstanding job with its women's initiative. Colleen Caden, chair of the firm's immigration practice and member of the executive committee, and Dyan Finguerra-DuCharme, a commercial litigator who focuses on intellectual property, are the two partners who lead Pryor Cashman's Women's Leadership Initiative. Colleen joined the firm as a lateral and saw the need for an initiative that focused on retaining and fostering the growth of women. In 2010, Colleen asked Ronald Shechtman, managing partner of Pryor Cashman, if the firm would invest in creating an initiative to support the development of women attorneys. He said "yes," without a moment's hesitation. Dyan took on the role as Colleen's co-chair shortly after she joined the firm in 2012.

"A critical key to the success of the program has been that the entire firm wholeheartedly supports the mission of the program, from the Executive Committee to every male and female attorney at the firm," explains Colleen. "The fact that we have been able to build a dynamic program is a direct result of the firm's active participation and steadfast support."

What makes Pryor Cashman's Women's Leadership Initiative so special is how hands-on it is. Its activities are grounded in the objective of empowering women lawyers by investing in their professional development. And Pryor Cashman is one of those firms that is making great strides in advancing women leaders, with several women partners in firm leadership positions, including on the compensation committee and as department heads.

Part of the Women's Leadership Initiative involves holding regular meetings open to all women lawyers and women senior administrative staff. At times, the meetings are informal and the group may get together without having a structured agenda. Other times, the meetings feature specific topics, from honing business development approaches to further developing oral advocacy to providing guidance as to how women can position themselves for board positions.

While the program attracts a range of guest speakers, some are taken from the firm's ranks and others are noted authors. The focus on business development included a talk from *Work It* author Carrie Kerpen, who discussed various approaches to being your authentic self and finding one's personal style in approaching new business and work, and another, by Pryor Cashman's own in-house chief marketing officer, Mike Mellor. "Every associate needs support and mentoring," says Dyan. "And with women, it's not just because of a gender line. Women are thinking about business development and building their practices, and we want to help them market themselves."

In collaboration with the firm's marketing department's help, Pryor Cashman publishes *Progress in Print*, a quarterly newsletter expressly produced for distribution to the firm's women attorneys. While links to the newsletter appear on the firm's website, the primary objective for the project is to help inform and encourage additional communications among women lawyers. It features a monthly message from Dyan and Colleen, news about upcoming events, and updates on recent activities by the firm's female lawyers, including speaking engagements and appearances in the press.

Dyan says, "The initiative has developed in a way where it has created a supportive forum for women to discuss issues, and so lawyers come to both Colleen and myself, with a host of topics. We want to give them guidance as mentors. We can help them navigate any of the types of typical law firm politics or a workload issue on a confidential basis. Our immediate goal is to foster communications and make women more self-confident. We want them to know that Pryor Cashman is a place where one can have these types of discussions."

What to Do?

Consultants point out that training and coaching can be beneficial in terms of getting both women and men to learn how to market more effectively, but given the fact that women still represent a small percentage of the largest rainmakers in any firm, women benefit from additional and often more focused training. Susan Saltonstall Duncan of Rainmaking Oasis, has conducted workshops, training sessions, and coaching for law firms throughout the country, including multiple programs dedicated specifically to women. She is an avid believer in training and coaching, but says that it is also important for women to take responsibility for and actively direct their own advancement. "To have control over your destiny by creating and finding your own path with the people who will advance you and support you is a must. Decide what it is you want your practice to be in five or ten years, what kind of clients you want to work with, who in the firm is apt to collaborate and help you succeed, and then be strategic about how you go about building and executing your plan, knowledge and skill set, and growing your own business," she says.

Based on multiple Legal Sales and Service Organization (LSSO) studies she has directed on women lawyers and business development issues, former corporate counsel and consultant Catherine Alman MacDonagh has identified four things that the more successful women rainmakers do to achieve great practices:

1.   **Have the right attitude.** Keep in mind that it is essential to recognize your successes. "Leverage your success and learn from your failures."

2.   **Take the lead.** "The most successful women business developers take on leadership roles inside and outside the firm. From the time they are associates, they should pursue and embrace opportunities to serve on committees and in leadership roles in business groups and legal associations."

3.   **Invest time wisely.** When volunteering, women should be intelligent about how they spend their time. "We've asked women, 'what activities do you engage in most?' Then, 'which activities gave the best results?' The activities they engaged in did not always produce the best results, and that gave us more of a roadmap. Diagnosing those things can be valuable."

4. **Successful women overcome barriers.** "In all our studies, the barriers identified were things like firm structure, lack of training, or lack of time. It didn't matter, the successful women we've studied figured out how to overcome those obstacles."

Think Piece

Ten Things Women in Law Can Do to Build Their Practice

By Bonnie P. Ciaramella*

To be successful and rise to the top of the law firm pyramid, it's not enough to do great work. Partners who bring in more business command better compensation and roles in firm leadership. Women lawyers need to do great work and take consistent steps to confidently network and build their personal brand. Clients are asking and expecting to see women lawyers on their matters; the time is right for women to be assertive in their professional outreach. Here are a few suggestions to get you started:

1.   Make networking a habit — like going to the gym. It's difficult to achieve success at most things if you are simply dabbling in them when things are slower. Challenge yourself to be focused and set weekly goals that fit in with your schedule, such as lunch with a client, prospect, referral source, or industry expert twice a week. It beats eating in your office and it keeps you current regarding market developments.

2.   Expand your network with relevant "warm" contacts. For example, review your law school graduating class and connect through LinkedIn with acquaintances and send a personal note to anyone with whom you were close and lost touch. If they reside in your city, ask them to coffee or lunch (see #1 above). If they reside

---

*   Bonnie Ciaramella is an experienced business strategist who works with law firm partners and executive teams to effect change and improve performance. She founded Ciaramella & Co. in 2004, a strategy consulting firm focused on improving the competitive position and market share of law firms.

in another city, add them to your list of people you will visit next time you are in their city.

3.   To build lasting relationships, be exceptionally professional, discreet, and thoughtful throughout your career. Make that part of your personal brand and take time to do small things—send a handwritten note, a thoughtful email, or a funny gift to memorialize an incident. Think of ways in which other professionals have made you feel special and be inspired in doing for others.

4.   Hire and train an assistant who will represent you well and go the extra mile when you need it most. You ideally want someone who supports you in handling your daily work, business contacts, scheduling, and family obligations. The right assistant, with your personal coaching and recognition, will help you achieve more with less effort.

5.   Identify internal opportunities to grow your business development and leadership skills. If you see an interesting project, don't wait to be asked. Start the conversation with the right people and let people know of your interest in joining a firm committee or women's initiative. As you increase your internal profile, more opportunities will come your way.

6.   Value critical feedback and learn how to use it to continually improve. Make a point of directly asking how and in what ways you can improve and in which areas you may need development. Clients and partners value lawyers who genuinely welcome feedback and learn from it.

7.   Take the initiative to identify and develop effective mentors (internal and external) and sponsors to help you to progress within the organization and get more client opportunities. Attend relevant internal meetings and take note of which partners are in leadership roles and asked to spearhead important firm initiatives.

8.   Identify at least one relevant industry, university, civic or nonprofit organization that interests you and become a vital and

active member. Time is limited, so choose an organization where you can make a real commitment and contribution, such as serving on a committee. This will enable people to see your abilities in action and expand your network.

9.   Learn and use relevant tools — such as an active LinkedIn profile — to make networking with contacts that much easier and more engaging. Work with your firm's PR staff to consider where and when you should author content on various subjects and expand your professional network through social media.

10.   And, of course, continue doing exceptional legal work each day to exceed expectations. Happy clients are great sources of referrals!

Chapter 10

The Future of Business Development and Legal Marketing

During the process of interviewing sources for this book, I spoke with more than sixty experts. They are an incredibly talented group consisting of lawyers, consultants, recruiters and marketers. Each one was selected because they exemplified some of the most interesting perspectives and best practices in the field of legal marketing.

After conducting these interviews, several consistent themes seemed to weave themselves throughout the content I was gathering. Here are four of the strongest that I believe may be shaping where the profession of legal marketing is headed. I have also included examples of two firms employing many of the best practices to get themselves to the future.

Some Key Themes

1.   **Relationship building is key in any business, but it's particularly critical in one so nuanced and dependent on the element of trust as the practice of law.** Relationships between lawyers and their clients, lawyers and their marketing staff, and lawyers with

one another within a partnership, are keys to success. Strong relationships remain the holy grail of business. The culture of a firm can make or break the organization, and it is also clear that those law firms with the strongest and most consistent culture — where their leadership communicates up and down the organization — are the most successful and often the most profitable. Building an environment supported by a compensation system that rewards business development yet encourages collaboration, is vital.

2.   **The legal landscape is changing due to the pace of technology, demands made by a newer generation of clients and the rise of ambitious business ventures.** In addition to the traditional organizations such as the International Bar Association and the American Bar Association, there are newer organizations such as the dynamic Corporate Legal Operations Consortium (CLOC) and Buying Legal Council to provoke essential discussions on operations and pricing. Companies such as Thomson Reuters, UnitedLex, Integreon and many of the accounting firms are also creating change by growing like plants into the technology voids that exist. Most law firms are just trying to keep pace.

Technology is impacting both the practice of law and the way marketing is done. Systems can assist marketing departments in streamlining their work so that staffers can work on more high-value activities, rather than keying in data and recycling new business pitches.

Tim Smith, the founder of OnePlace, a Client Relationship Management system built specifically for legal and accounting firms on the Salesforce platform, explains how technology can be shaped to allow lawyers to track client activity and relationships, referrals, matters and billing information, experience and CV changes, opportunities (potential deals), etc., available through automated workflows all at the touch of a finger. OnePlace links to the law firm's client network so that a lawyer on her way to a client can access contacts and company information on her phone, including any fees paid to the firm by the client, and prepare a new business pitch. After the meeting, OnePlace also reminds the lawyer to provide the system with feedback from the meeting. It triggers her to dictate into her phone any significant notes and suggested follow-up items. These meeting notes are also sent to other lawyers who preselected to keep tabs on the contact or the results of the meeting.

Foundation Experience Management is another enterprise-software platform, but one that helps firms leverage their collective matters and other work experience as well as the lawyer's expertise, organized in one place so that it can be easily pulled by the marketing department and the firm's lawyers.

These new technologies are raising the bar as well as client expectations, for all law firms.

3.   Marketing legal services has been around long enough so that best practices surrounding the operations of marketing departments have been demystified. Amanda Brady of Major Lindsey says, "The CMOs out in the field are changing and we're seeing an evolution. There is now an expectation that they are commercially minded, understand the business of the firm, and contribute to the larger conversation regarding the firm's business strategy and position in the marketplace. In order to be successful, they have to be brought in and be involved at the firm-wide level and the practice level in order to effectuate what needs to be done. It is the only way that they can hope to develop and implement plans that will be meaningful and relevant to the organization."

Coaching by experienced salespeople and building marketing departments in tandem with professionals with proven track records is now seen as a must. Advice on everything from search engine optimization to predictive analytics is now easy to access. Law firm leaders are growing marketing departments as they recognize that these resources are an integral part of operating a business, not an ancillary back-office operation. Most partners see the value in partnering with marketers to maximize their practices' growth potential. They are no longer afraid to hire outside consultants to help guide them in terms of staffing issues or marketing plans, or individual leadership coaches in leadership and business development skills.

Best practices within firms are also being assisted by targeted modern tech tools. Adam Stock, the Chief Information Officer of Allen Matkins Leck Gamble Mallory & Natsis LLP, thinks newer technology will allow firms to score leads and contacts so that they can see which ones have higher value. "Hubspot, Marketo and Gwabbit, are just a few of the technologies that can do this," says Adam. "As a CMO, you can tell if 'Bill' came to the firm as a client, but you can't easily see if Bill was actively giving us business prior to this point, or which partners had interacted with Bill in the past, or the strength of those relationships. Now there is technology that allows you to see all of that in one place. We also have marketing systems to measure what is useful and what is not." If firms could use that information to make a 10% change in process improvement, or redirect some of their marketing efforts, they could make enormous strides.

4. With the disruption in the marketplace, many firms are searching for new identities. Most firms seem to be gravitating toward one of two axes. On one axis are firms that are laser-focused or boutique-like, such as Wilkinson Walsh; Gunderson Dettmer; or Macfarlanes. These are firms that position themselves as doing just a few things expertly well working in specific and defined markets. In those markets, they are recognized for handling the work exceptionally within a very high-touch practice. On the other axis are the mega-firms that innovate by trying for great efficiencies but still focus on a few core practice areas. Firms such as Allen & Overy; Orrick; and Dentons are leading the way on this path. The day of the supermarket one-shop-fits-all law firm is over. In-house counsel want to hire specialists. Quality of the delivery will also be evaluated with the use of AI, so that the technology that is part of the solution may also become part of the evaluation.

According to Charles Martin of Macfarlanes, "In the future, it will be even tougher to occupy the premium end of the market than it is today. There are many firms that believe they should be on that patch, yet some will need to set their sights on something different. Valuable but different."

The bifurcation of the market is nothing new. Those of us who study the *American Lawyer*'s Am Law 100 list have seen the changes. Barry Wolf of Weil Gotshal says "There are these incredibly profitable firms, about fifteen of them, and then there is a huge drop off to those with a much lower profit per partner. The problem is that once you fall far from that top tier, you can't go back up. The biggest challenge is keeping your level of profitability high while maintaining a solid culture."

While the firm landscape is bifurcating, entities investing in technology have entered the market. "If law firms don't invest in the technology to do things faster, better or cheaper, other businesses will step in," says Charles. "Let's say ten years ago, out of all of a client's legal requirements, maybe one-half were satisfied by external law firms, one-third by their own in-house counsel, and the rest, handled by a mixed bag of other people, like those from the big four accounting firms. Today, that looks very different, with in-house counsel handling a greater share. Traditional law firms will be a smaller part of the cake."

Henry Nassau of Dechert recounts the sentiment from a recent roundtable gathering of heads of law firms and said, "When I left, I knew that the general consensus was that big changes are coming. While none of us know with certainty where it is coming from, and for now life is great, we all have our eyes on our clients and on changes on the horizon. As Bill Gates said, 'We always overestimate the change that will occur in two years and underestimate the change that will occur in the next ten. Don't let yourself be lulled into inaction.'"[1]

---

1.   Bill Gates, The Road Ahead (Viking Penguin 1995).

Two Examples of Firms Employing Best Practices

Two firms that have adapted to many of these principles are Orrick, Herrington & Sutcliffe LLP and Gunderson Dettmer Stough Villeneuve Franklin & Hachigian, LLP, but with very different approaches. Gunderson Dettmer is succeeding for its disciplined focus on doing just a few things at the pinnacle of performance, involving associates in the core of the business, and demonstrating in numerous ways that its actions as a firm are consistent with its principles. Orrick is large, with more than 1,000 lawyers and twenty-five offices. It is digging in deep to explore new uses of technology and collaboration. The firm was recently named one of *Fortune's* Best Companies to Work For, and in both 2016 and 2017, the *Financial Times'* Most Innovative Law Firm. Interestingly, both firms have their roots in California's Bay Area.

Gunderson Dettmer

Gunderson Dettmer is a high-caliber law firm representing more than 2,500 high-growth technology and life science companies and 250 of the world's leading venture capital firms. Launched in 1995 by a group of former partners who left the now-defunct Brobeck, Phleger & Harrison, including Bob Gunderson and Scott Dettmer, the firm has an intense focus on one thing — the venture capital world. Representing entrepreneurs and more VC funds than any other firm in the world, it is one of the small handful of law firms that Silicon Valley's talented entrepreneurs contact when they want to grow and access capital. Clients generally approach Gunderson Dettmer lawyers when they are in the earlier part of their company's entrepreneurial lifecycle and just getting started. But most are so engaged with the firm, they remain with the firm throughout their growth, often past an IPO.

Bob Gunderson is a business school graduate whose father worked for Procter & Gamble and shared with Bob many of the key lessons of classic marketing. Bob says, "I learned early on that you want to be number one in all of the markets you are in."

"I think we've tried to be extremely consistent in showing what we value. If it's a value, then we need to live it."

—Robert V. Gunderson, Gunderson Dettmer Stough Villeneuve Franklin & Hachigian, LLP

When the Gunderson Dettmer partners launched the firm, they decided to focus on just those things at which they could excel. They wanted to cement their reputation as the very best in a particular area, so from the very beginning they needed to differentiate themselves from other firms.

Venture was and is a very vibrant field with a set of activities that are interrelated: advising entrepreneurs, helping them raise capital often through venture fund investment and subsequently possibly selling themselves, or launching an IPO. Gunderson Dettmer represents these entrepreneurs but also a majority of the country's leading VC funds in their own activities. This constant synergy of the various aspects of raising capital and helping promising companies develop provides the firm with a holistic view of the venture capital ecosystem.

"Doing just a few things exceptionally well means turning down business," says Bob. "We don't want to be in a situation where we're offering services where we don't believe we really are the best. We only want to do what we are best at doing. In addition, it's hard to have an integrated firm if you have practices with widely different profit margins."

"We've seen law firms over-expand and go beyond their reach. If that happened at a conglomerate, they might say, 'Hey, this is not an area that's growing sufficiently for our stockholders to be happy,' and they would shed the business," says Bob. "I think it shows discipline in the sense of re-evaluating. I'm not sure it's easy for law firms to do this, but you have continuously to ask yourself if you are in the right spaces."

Bob also points out that cross-selling is not an issue for them. "It's easy to do if your partner in that area really is the best, but if they are not and you've suggested the client work with them, then have you done right by your client? And while firms often incentivize cross-selling, it's tough to put into actual action."

You notice what is different about Gunderson Dettmer as soon as you walk into their office. In both San Francisco and Redwood City (Silicon Valley) you know you are not inside a prototypical law firm: lots of open space, most walls are glass, and in the center is "the bullpen," where partners and associates work together, each with a double-screen set-up. Clear-walled offices, each of the same size, are located around the perimeter. You are not sure if you've entered an Apple store or a CSI lab.

Bob said he was inspired to approach the space differently when he visited another local firm in the mid-1990s. "I walked in and the receptionist was cowering behind a desk that looked more like an expensive wooden fortress. It was about four or five feet high. From a client's point of view, I thought it looked both expensive and unwelcoming."

When it came time for Bob and his partners to design their space, they decided they wanted to look more like a software company than a law firm. "No wood paneling," said Bob, but instead he insisted that the designer — who was more well-known for doing tech companies than law firms — use clear glass so that everyone could look around the office to see their colleagues. While all lawyers can decide to work in a singular office or the bullpen area, most choose the more open and collaborative option. It's a firm that encourages partners and associates to work closely with one another and for associates to go out on their own to develop their own book of business.

Bob points out that when the partners developed the design of the space, they wanted to do whatever they could to avoid the typical hierarchies found within law firms. "Partners, senior associates, junior associates — everybody's got the same-sized office. Being fair, treating everyone the same, is fundamental to our values. It's one of those things where lots of times, people say, 'Oh, I believe in this and that.' But there will be little clues, things that are inconsistent, that show you that while they say one thing, they actually do another. I think we've tried to be extremely consistent in showing what we value. If it's a value, then we need to live it."

Orrick

Ralph Baxter at Orrick was known to many in the legal profession as one of the great law firm visionaries. He led Orrick's transformation from a San Francisco regional firm to a leading global platform and established the first law firm offsite consolidated operations center, in Wheeling, West Virginia.

In 2013, Mitch Zuklie, a former Director of Venture Law Group LLP and a partner in the firm's venture capital practice, took the reins, charged with creating a strategy that would carry the firm to the next stage of evolution. Mitch knew that he needed to think out of the box and listen to a lot of perspectives at the firm, at clients, and in the market. He says, "I knew this had to come out of our collective efforts. And I have the benefit of being a guy who practiced in the tech space. My whole professional career has been working with innovative tech companies. It has come in handy in this role."

Part of the new strategy was to be sector-focused in three critical areas: technology, energy and infrastructure, and finance. By doing this, all of the firm's offices are primarily producing similar work. For Orrick, having that commonality or similar experience is essential to the business model, to building a distinctive brand, and integrating the firm. It allows the firm to provide comparable services across a platform and make investments that make sense across clients in a way that wouldn't be possible if the firm tried to do all things for all people.

Another element of the strategy was to excel on innovation. The firm defines innovation by focusing on delivering ever-increasing levels of value and service to its clients. Mitch says, "It's clear to us that if we don't innovate, and we don't change and we don't get more efficient, we're not going to be relevant in five years."

The firm recently launched Orrick Labs, an in-house team of technologists dedicated to accelerating the development of customized technology solutions.

They also have created a team of people and products called Orrick Analytics, which disaggregates tasks that can be performed with greater accuracy, efficiency, and security by using technology, project management discipline, and specialist lawyers and staff. The Orrick Analytics team, much of it based in the West Virginia Center, draws on a full toolkit of search, AI and other technologies. Once an administrative back office, today the center houses large teams of lawyers and staff who are an integral part of client-service teams.

In addition, the firm recognizes the need to communicate and engage lawyers and staff at all levels in innovating. To engage partners, the firm asks all partners to spend 2% of their time each year innovating and making the firm stronger. They call it "2% Time" projects, and partners describe how they plan to use the time in their individual business plans each year. Last year, Mitch convened a group of twenty partners with only one or two years of partnership experience — known as the Higgins Commission — to advise the Board on the firm's five-year strategy. They looked at clients, collaboration, talent and innovation. The firm gives associates fifty hours of credit each year for working on innovation-related projects. All lawyers and staff are eligibile for a $50,000 Innovation

Prize each year. And the firm's Chief Innovation Officer regularly leads hackathons at retreats and office events.

"Our last partnership retreat," says Mitch, "had a three-word theme: listen, collaborate and innovate. During that weekend, we spent a lot of time listening to audio clips of clients describing why some of the themes resonate with them, why we're hitting the right notes with them and what they need from us in the future. It was designed to spur on the discussion and bring our clients' perspectives into our internal dialogue."

Mitch says that everybody in the firm, whether a partner, an associate or a staff member, understands the strategy. Everyone who starts at the firm, on their first day gets an email from him describing the long-term strategy and core values and why innovation is important at Orrick. "And we talk about our progress toward that strategy at every quarterly town hall meeting, in monthly 'good, bad & ugly' reports to partners, and every leadership discussion."

The firm is also focused on promoting collaboration. Mitch notes, "The most important question the Board asks as part of our annual performance review and compensation process is not 'what did you do?' It's 'Who's been most helpful to you in achieving your goals?' and the people who get the most meaningful mentions from others around the firm get a special cash bonus and a lot of recognition from their peers."

Maybe it's not a surprise that the two firms used as prime examples for their collections of best practices have entrepreneurial California roots. Perhaps by acting more like start-ups, and not taking anything for granted, all law firms can take on more of an entrepreneurial focus. By taking this approach and remembering that we are in a service business where change is a constant, we can continue to look for new ways to create more value and help ourselves and our clients.

Index

(References are to pages.)

A

B

C

Culture of firm (*cont'd*)
   marketer's role in, 61–62
   new hires, effect on culture of, 57
   sharing and growing (cross-selling) clients, 69–70
   training, culture of, 62–63, 71

D

Day, Lara, 61
Dewey, Katrina, 126
Diaferia, Jamie, 116, 128, 135, 138, 141
Directories, listing in, 124–27
Dressler, Rachel, 1
Duncan, Susan Saltonstall, 103, 161

E

Electronic bidding, 14–15
Eskovitz, Sean, 117
Events for clients, prospects and referral sources, hosting, 123–24

F

Feldman, Sally, 114, 118
Ferrara, Ralph, 38–39, 41, 56, 120
Finguerra-DuCharme, Dyan, 159–60
Finkelstein, Jerry, 7
Franke, Jeffrey, 19
Friendships with clients, 42, 44, 47

G

H

I

K

L

N

O

P

Q

R

S

T